OBSERVATIONS
ON THE
BILL FOR THE REGULATION AND IMPROVEMENT OF COMMONS.
1876.

BY CHARLES ELTON,
OF LINCOLN'S INN, BARRISTER-AT-LAW,

Author of "The Tenures of Kent," "The Law of Commons and Waste Lands," and "The Law of Copyholds and Customary Tenures."

LONDON:

WILDY AND SONS,

LINCOLN'S INN ARCHWAY, W.C.

MEREDITH, RAY, & LITTLER, MANCHESTER.

1876.

CONTENTS.

Chapter I.

COMMONS AND WASTES.

SCOPE of Bill.—Definition of Commons.—Varieties of ancient tenure in Common Lands.—Manorial Wastes.—What are Rights of Common.—Manors and their Origin.—Tenants' Rights on Wastes.—Different Kinds of Wastes.—Strips by Roads.—Sea-Shore.—Village Greens.—Their Nature and Origin.—Early Example of Rights of Recreation.—Public Recreation Grounds.—Legal Fictions.—Royal Forests. — Definition. — Commoners' Rights.—Survivals of old tenures in Forests.—Rights of Tinbounders.—Similar Customs . . ' . Page 1

Chapter II.

COMMON FIELDS.

Nature of Common Fields.—Origin of Common-Field Husbandry.—Distribution by Lot.—Early Separation of Arable and Pasture.—Arable rarely Distributed by Lot.—Earliest Forms of Common Husbandry in England.—

Evils of Common Husbandry.—Act of 1773.—Instances of Evils.—Opinions of Eminent Authorities.—Classification of Commonable Lands.—Shack Fields.—Intermixed Arable Fields.—Lammas Lands.—Stinted Pastures.—Commonable Woodlands.—Lot Meadows . Page 24

CHAPTER III.

INCLOSURES.

Disputes as to Commons and Wastes.—Approvement. —Early Inclosures.—Statute of Merton.—Open Spaces Committee. — Means of Securing Public Recreation Ground.—Disputes as to Common Fields.—Changes in System of Agriculture.—Effect of Inclosures and Changing Arable to Pasture.—Rebellions.—Local Inclosure Acts.—Lord Worsley's Act.—Open Spaces round London. —Early Complaints of Growth of London.—Decay of Archery.—Riots.—Proclamations against Building.—The Metropolitan Commons Acts.—Memorandum of Inclosure Commissioners . . . . . Page 42

CHAPTER IV.

PROVISIONS OF THE BILL.

Objects of Bill.—Method of Procedure.—What Lands are Included.—Definitions.—Applications to Commissioners.—Who are Persons Interested.—Consents how to be given.—Compensation on Inclosure.—Saving of

Contents. vii

Manorial Rights, whether required.—Customary Rights of Miners, whether to be Protected.—Regulation of Commons by General Inclosure Act.—New Provisions.—Improvement of Commons.—Old Powers of Improvement, whether to be Abolished.—Regulation of Commons which do not come under the Act.—Estates and Interests of Owners and Commoners.—Whether they can be acquired for the public benefit.—What Provisions would be necessary . . . . . . Page 64

APPENDIX.

The Commons Bill, 1876 . . Page 93

Chapter I.

COMMONS AND WASTES.

Scope of Bill.—Definition of Commons.—Varieties of ancient tenure in common lands.—Manorial wastes.—What are rights of common.—Manors and their origin.—Tenant's rights on wastes.—Different kinds of wastes.—Strips by roads.—Sea-shore.—Village greens.—Their nature and origin.—Early example of rights of recreation.—Public recreation grounds.—Legal fictions.—Royal forests. — Definition. — Commoner's rights. — Survivals of old tenures in forests. — Rights of tin-bounders. — Similar customs.

THE Bill for the Regulation and Inclosure of Commons is a measure of very simple form, but its subject is thrice-vexed and intricate in the highest degree. The word "common" does not only apply to places like Hampstead Heath or Putney Green, but includes all kinds of places where ancient rights impede the freedom of cultivation. And not only is it difficult to define the subject-matter of the Bill, but the very principles on which the measure rests are subjects of doubt and debate. A powerful party opposes the measure in Parliament, on the ground that it allows inclosures to be made by all kinds of persons: it is urged that when the lord and commoners are all agreed, the Bill provides no protection against private and vexatious inclosures; while outside the House it has received praise on all sides as the best exposition of a new principle, that no inclosure is ever to be made without the formal sanction of Parliament.

The main object of the Bill is to enable the Inclosure Commissioners to make provisional orders for inclosing or regulating "commons" according to local requirements, the orders having no validity until confirmed by Parliament. The Act is to apply to all lands which could hitherto have been inclosed under the General Act of 1845, comprising all kinds of lands where different classes of persons have rights and interests in the soil or its natural produce, as well as "the bare-worn common" of ordinary life.

We live in England among the *débris* of many systems of law; and it is not surprising, therefore, that the list of "commons" should include many strange varieties of property, some originating in feudal times, and many dating from a prehistoric antiquity, as to which we must hope that by due legal process they may shortly disappear. In the meantime they possess a certain practical interest, not merely for the owners of such estates and rights, but also for the State; for public policy has been much impeded by the existence of these primitive estates and interests, founded on the rules of antique societies and trammelled by vexatious usages, of which the origin is for the most part forgotten.

The lands which are the subject of the Bill, may be conveniently divided into two principal classes; the first comprising all manorial wastes, and the second all commonable fields, meadows and woods, and lands where the soil and the herbage or wood are the property of different owners.

But before proceeding to describe the land in each of these divisions, it will be better to say what is meant by the expression "commoners' rights." These rights are of several kinds, differing widely in their origin and in their present extent, and it is not easy to frame a definition which shall cover all their varieties, preserving at the same time the legal distinction between the interest of a commoner and the separate estate which a person or class of persons may have in some particular produce of the soil. One man, for instance, may have the coals in a certain place, another all the stone, another the thorns and brushwood, and another the rest of the estate, and none of them will be commoners. Or the corporation of a borough may be the owners of a tract of pasture like Port Meadow near Oxford, and every burgess may be entitled to feed so many cattle there, and yet none of them are commoners or ever have been such: for many boroughs have held their property from the time when they were free townships of an invading German tribe. Or we might take the case of Alnwick Moor, where the soil belongs to the lord of the borough, and the freemen of Alnwick have or had each the privilege of feeding so many cows and so many sheep, and to cut turf and bushes and get slate and building stone from the open quarries; and these are not rights of common, because no one else is allowed to share the right; and nothing is left for the owner of the soil. Perhaps a commoner's interest may be most conveniently described as a right to take for his own use part of the produce of another man's land, the landowner being entitled to all that the commoner does not take. The commoner's right may exhaust the whole value of the property, or in another case may be of a very trifling kind. He may have the privilege of feeding a horse in a field, or of turning his sheep upon a moor, or pigs into an oak-wood, or he may be entitled to pasture all his live stock upon the herbage of a meadow or stubble. And according to the circumstances of the case, a class of tenants or a single person may have the power of taking peat or coal for fuel, timber for repairs, and shrubs and fern for littering cattle, rabbits, wildfowl, or fish for food, stone and gravel for building, and so on in a great variety of instances. There seems to be hardly any limit to the possible variations of these rights, which in one place may be nearly valueless and in another are almost as good as a freehold estate.

We will now proceed to the description of the places where these rights of common may be used.

Manorial Wastes.

A manor is a district in which a "lord" has or had jurisdiction over his tenants, and in many cases over all persons residing there, and who enjoys among other privileges the ownership of all waste lands to which no one else in the district can make out a title in the ordinary way. In courts of law the fiction prevails that the king was once the absolute owner of the country, and that he gave this particular district to the ancestors of the lord of the manor, to deal with as they pleased; whereupon they gave part to their fighting-men so long as they should behave well in the wars, another part to the Church, that the priests might pray for their souls, another portion to the free labourers and serfs who were to cultivate the lord's private domain, and all the rest they kept for themselves. And so it happens that for the last thousand years "the lord is the owner of everything upwards to heaven and downwards to the centre of the earth," except such things as custom, usage, and grant have conferred upon tenants and commoners. But, turning to the field of history, we find that the original manors were districts which we call by that name when speaking of the tenants, or townships when we regard the inhabitants, or parishes in matters ecclesiastical. We cannot of course determine the nature in each instance of the district which the manor now represents: "a township (says Professor Stubbs) may represent the original allotment of the smallest subdivision of the free community, or the settlement of the kindred colonising on their own account, or the estate of the great proprietor who has a tribe of dependents;" and he remarks, that those early townships which were founded on the land of a lord were, in many respects, much the same as manors from the beginning of English history. In course of time the free communities fell into the power of the Crown or the greater landowners, and the process appears to have been almost complete before the Norman Conquest. Since that date the waste grounds have belonged to the lords of the manors, except where the corporation of a city or borough has managed to retain its common property, or where a class of manorial tenants has, after long struggles, succeeded in proving that they have always excluded the lord from a particular piece of land, or reduced him to take a specific share of the produce.

Upon the wastes of a manor the tenants of freehold and copyhold lands have the right to feed as many cattle as their lands will sustain in winter, or some specific number of cattle, according to the usage; and according to the custom of some districts, one part of the wastes may be appropriated to the freeholders, and another to the copyhold tenants. Besides this ordinary right, any tenant or set of tenants may have the right to take so much as they require of the other produce of the land. Under the name of "estovers," for instance, a man may be entitled, subject to the rules prevailing in the particular district, to allowances of wood and underwood or shrubs for domestic and agricultural purposes. Under this title he may claim timber-trees for building, or the under-boughs or tops and lops of trees and windfalls for fuel or for mending his ploughs and waggons, or for making gates and fences, or for other farm necessities. Or he may have the right of "turbary," which entitles him to take peat fit for burning in his house; and so, according to the usage, he can claim various other privileges so long as they are not exercised in a capricious or unreasonable manner, and are confined to the needs of the commoner as owner of a particular house or piece of land.

Under the name of "wastes," several different kinds of land may be included. There will be the rough pasture or moor, or it may be a tract of sheep-down, which from ancient times has been devoted to the needs of the tenants, or, as happens sometimes, to the use of a particular class of tenants; this may represent either the common pasture of some free community of old times, usurped in times of war by the thane or baron who gained the lordship of the district, or in perhaps the greater number of cases, it represents the vacant land which a church or a nobleman, obtaining a grant of "folk-land," allotted to the serfs, whose system of husbandry was, in everything except ownership, carefully modelled upon that of the free villages. It has been most clearly pointed out by Sir Henry Maine, that similar forms of ownership do not show that the owners' rights had an identity of origin. "The ancient type of ownership long served as the model for tenancy, and the common holdings, dying out as property, survived as occupations." And in a great number of instances it can be shown, that the rights of common, which look like survivals from a time when the land belonged to the villagers, are in reality privileges which an absolute owner gave to his tenants, when he founded a dependent community on the model of those townships where the freemen were the collective owners of the district.

Besides the commons where the tenants enjoy their rights of pasture, "the wastes" include the strips of land by the sides of roads, stretching from one piece of common to another, which are held to belong to the lord of the manor, because his ancestors probably made the road, and roads in early times were driven through the waste-lands of manors, avoiding the old inclosures. And where the manor fronts upon the sea, the beach and shore will be included in the wastes, the commoners in many places having rights of taking sand and seaweed for use upon their holdings; and in more cases than the Crown is always willing to acknowledge, the foreshores down to the ordinary low-water mark belong to the lord of the manor, or persons deriving their title through him; and in some districts even the bed of the sea or of an estuary for some distance from land has been shown to belong to the subject, notwithstanding the *primâ facie* title of the Crown to all below the average high-water mark.

The village green, too, is usually part of the waste, although from its peculiar nature the property in this part of the common is of no use to the nominal owner. The green has been often described, but very rarely defined, and in many a popular speech the merits of the green have been attributed to the common pastures, and even to the intermixed fields of a township. In a most valuable course of lectures, for instance, which were published by the Professor of Political Economy at Cambridge, we find the following statements: "Formerly there was scarcely a parish in England which had not its common. This was, as its name implies, a tract of land which was the joint property of all the inhabitants of the village: here they could graze a cow or feed poultry, and here too was a recreation-ground so delightful, that the pleasures of the village green have been immortalized by some of our greatest poets. Unfortunately, in the year 1836, an Act of Parliament was passed with the view of facilitating the inclosure of commons. The commons are being rapidly swept away. Cottagers have now no means of keeping a cow, a pig, or poultry; the village games are gone: . . .

and I have been too often pained to find that the turnpike-road is now the only recreation-ground for village children." This is in one point an evident reminiscence of Goldsmith: and in fact the sweet, though unhistorical strains of the "Deserted Village," are usually accepted as the best exposition of the law of village greens. But in real life it seldom happens that

> "Amidst the bowers the tyrant's hand is seen,
> And desolation saddens all the green."

The village green is generally described by legal writers as a small open space, dedicated by immemorial custom to the recreation of the villagers; but in some places the inhabitants have similar rights over playing fields, which do not belong to the lord of the manor. It is not every piece of Nomansland, where strangers have rambled or boys and girls played games, that can claim the immunities of a village green; there must be *bonâ fide* evidence that for a long time the place has been appropriated to the amusement of the inhabitants of a particular district. Nor, on the other hand, is it necessary to show that special kinds of games have always been played by the villagers: for so the Courts might be involved in problems respecting the lawfulness of balloon-ball, which was forbidden by Edward III., or of bowls, which were unlawful to the meaner sort of men, unless they could get a licence from a gentleman with a hundred a year; and difficult questions might arise as to the mode of conducting a cricket match in the reign of Richard I. It is rarely that difficulties occur in practice respecting the liberties of the village greens; but it is somewhat remarkable that so little should be known of their origin and early history. We have reason to believe that England was in some early time like Sir Thomas More's "Utopia," where "no man was idle, and yet no man worked as if he were an ass from morning unto night: for the Utopians laboured but six hours in the day, and gave the rest to honest recreation;" but what with the statutes for the encouragement of archery and the abolition of idle games, and the change of habits that may be traced to Puritan influence, most of the village sports have long since come to an end. The earliest account of a village green which appears in the law-books is believed to be one relating to a common playing-place in a parish in Essex, to which a piece of copyhold land was added in 1496, the conveyance of which contained a mention of the rights of recreation on the green which the lord of the manor had granted to the villagers in ancient times; and the tenant was directed to permit the archers and players of games in the village to use and enjoy their sports according to the ancient usage, without any let or hindrance ("*permittendo architenentes sagittarios et lusores villæ prædictæ ibidem habere uti et gaudere joca sua more solito et consueto absque impedimento seu vexatione*"). There have been some proposals of late years to extend the doctrine of village greens in a very curious way. It was thought that the commons and open fields round London might be secured as public greens by setting up a kind of national-local custom of rambling and playing at games—such as football and donkey-races,—and so the payment of compensation to private owners might be evaded by a legal fiction. One is reminded by this of the devices by which " that vile prerogative fellow Noy," and other jurists of his time obtained mines for the Crown; "the common law appropriates everything to the persons whom it best suits, as common and trivial things to the common people, and because gold and silver are most excellent things, the law has appointed them to the person who is most excellent, and that is the king;" and so when a title was wanted to the sea-shore, it was once found sufficient to allege that the shore is the waste of the king's manor of England whereon his tenants have only a public common of piscary. But it has been laid down by an eminent judge, that no Court will avail itself of legal fictions, invented in feudal times to support rights of property, as a means of destroying rights of ownership acquired by long-continued possession.

Before leaving the manorial waste, a few words may be said with respect to rights of common which are taken in royal forests, and certain rights of dealing with waste ground which prevail in mineral districts. A forest, according to its legal definition, is a territory with great woods for the secret abode of wild beasts, and fruitful pastures for their continual feeding, kept for the princely delight and pleasure of the king to hunt with his nobles for his recreation, when he is wearied with the burden of cares in matters of common-weal. It was the most odious part of the prerogative of our early Norman kings to extend their forests over the fields and pastures of their subjects, whose only recompense, besides the sense of ministering to the princely delight, was a right of common for such cattle as would not disturb the wild beasts, through all the open places in the forest. The villages in the precinct of the forest were called forest-towns, and the landowners in each township had the right of common to recompense them for the damage done by the deer and other game, "because the king's wild beasts had their continual haunt and repair to feed in quiet peace upon their lands." But if there was a disafforestation, or if any lands were withdrawn from the forest, this special right of common came to an end at once. The forest laws have recently been used with great effect for the discomfiture of persons who made inclosures on the strength of a crown-licence, without proper regard for the rights of the forest-commoners. However praiseworthy and public-spirited may have been the motives of the successful commoners, it is not easy to see how their victory can show the illegality of all inclosures in places where no wild beasts continually haunt and repair; and yet the assumption is by no means rarely made. As to the question of the public rights in the few forests which remain to the Crown, it has been said with much force, in the lectures before-cited, that though the deer have vanished, the proprietary rights of the Crown remain, and consequently the people represented by the Crown have considered it their undisputed privilege to walk through the pleasant glades, and to wander about undisturbed amid the forest scenery. But though this seems to be perfectly just with regard to Crown lands in the forest, it must still be remembered that every forest includes the lands of many private persons, whose ordinary rights of ownership are only limited by the necessity of providing for the comfort of the imaginary wild beasts; so that the statement as to the public rights of recreation must be taken with the necessary limitation.

From an historical point of view the royal forests are extremely interesting, because within their limits are found traces of early institutions, of which in other parts of the country the memory has almost died away. This has been noticed by historians on more than one occasion, with reference to Crown lands in general, "where customs are maintained to this day which recall the most primitive institutions;" and it seems likely, that in the troubled times before the Norman Conquest many free communities became direct tenants of the Crown, instead of falling under the neighbouring lords, and were permitted to retain their primitive usages, so long as in matters of revenue and forest-law they fulfilled their duty to the king. What could be more archaic than the manners and customs of the men of Pamber in Hampshire, whose court was held in a piece of ground called Lawday-mead, which belonged to the constable for the year, the proceedings being recorded by notches on square wooden tallies, and the first business of the court being the election of the lord of the manor, " to whom belonged stray cattle, &c., and who had the right of hunting and hawking as far as Windsor!" Another curious fragment of ancient law, preserved upon these royal domains, consists in the rights of the tin-bounders of Cornwall and Devonshire, and of the free-miners on the Mendip Hills, the High Peak, and the Forest of Dean. The rights differ in each of these localities in the mode of their exercise, the extent of the miners' rights, and the antique ceremonies and duties on which these rights depend, and in some of these districts they are regulated by local Acts of Parliament. But they all agree in their main character, being rights of searching upon waste grounds for tin, lead, iron, or calamine-stone, as the case may be, an inclosure being made in some symbolical way of so much land as the custom permits; the extent is sometimes limited by a definite measure, or sometimes as much as the miner, standing in his pit, could cover by throwing his rake in two directions, or as was once laid down in the language of the law, "*C'est bon custom en Derbyshire de foder plumbum in alieno solo auxi far qu'un home poet caster son spade vel his mattock.*" The space of land inclosed by the miner is described as "his mine with which he can do as he likes best: but if the lord of the manor will buy the mine and pay its value, he may have it before all other men." The usages of these miners seem to belong to a time when the mountain-wastes had not in any way been reduced into private ownership, and we can only find a parallel to them in such rights as that of owning the bed of the sea as far as the owner of the shore can see a Hamburgh barrel, or the ownership that might be gained under the law of the Ostrogoths "by shouting or throwing," in the sea by casting a spear from a boat with one end upon the shore, or in the woods by taking the land as far as the voice could be heard on a still night, the free-man standing on his own land and shouting into the forest. But whatever may be their origin, these rights of inclosing waste-lands for purposes of mining are still of practical value and importance, and in passing any measure, which deals generally with waste grounds, the miners' local rights will doubtless be considered.

Chapter II.

COMMON FIELDS.

Nature of Common Fields.—Origin of Common-field Husbandry.—Distribution by Lot.—Early Separation of Arable and Pasture.—Arable rarely Distributed by Lot.—Earliest Forms of Common Husbandry in England.—Evils of Common Husbandry.—Act of 1773.—Instances of Evils.—Opinions of Eminent Authorities.—Classification of Commonable Lands.—Shack Fields.—Intermixed Arable Fields.—Lammas Lands.—Stinted Pastures.—Commonable Woodlands.—Lot Meadows.

WE now come to the description of those commonable lands, which are "commons" within the meaning of the Bill, although they have been in actual cultivation under successive owners from the time when our country was first settled by its present inhabitants.

If we go back for a century we shall find that most of the cultivated land in England, especially where the earliest settlements were made, was laid out in open fields and pastures, such as the well-known Fordington Field, near Dorchester, containing 4,000 acres, where 1,300 acres of arable and a feeding-ground for 5,000 head of cattle have always been owned and managed by a small body of cultivators; and, notwithstanding all the inclosures which have been carried out in recent times, there are still to be found in many parts of the country various kinds of open fields and commonable grounds which form no part of any manorial waste. Living persons can recollect the time when a great part of England was covered with Trinity Fields and Lammas Lands, held in separate allotments during a close season, and thrown open either to all the severalty owners or to a larger class of commoners when the corn and hay were carried. These relics of the common-field husbandry are survivals from our earliest system of tenures. They date from a time when private property in arable land was barely disengaged from the collective ownership of the tribe, while the pasture lands and woods were still owned and occupied by all the villagers in common. It seems probable that private ownership of arable land prevailed among the earliest Teutonic settlers in this country, but the matter is not wholly free from doubt. On this point we may cite Professor Nasse, of Bonn, as the greatest living authority. While (he says) it can be plainly recognized that among the early German communities the house and farm-stead were private property, and pasture and woodland held in common, the extent to which arable land was common is more doubtful. "There seems early to have been a difference in this respect among different tribes. But the original state of things probably was that arable land was not held permanently as private property, but was from time to time redistributed among the community for temporary occupation by lot. Up to the most recent times there have been here and there districts in Germany, in which an annual repartition of all arable land took place among the community, and even now there are cases in which a portion of the arable is private property, another periodically allotted to or used by the members of a community in a certain rotation. In England also the periodic allotment of meadows and plots of arable land, which occasionally, though rarely, used to take place, points to a similar state of things. On the other hand, however, it is maintained by some, that such alterations in the occupation of land since the historic period were always exceptional, and that private possession of it has been the rule among the Germanic races ever since their appearance in history." And he pronounces for the opinion that the villagers used to select portions of land to be used in turn for arable through a period of years, and that when exhausted by several crops the land was laid in fallow, and for a long period was only used for pasture, a custom of husbandry which certainly long prevailed in Cornwall. "The regular cultivation of the same plots of land gradually made the periodic partition appear less desirable, and it became less and less frequent; among the Anglo-Saxons of the earliest historical times, the separation of arable and pasture, with permanent private possession of arable land, seems to have been the rule; but after the ancient system of agriculture had disappeared, the use of the land for centuries was regulated by certain rules for the public interest, and when the land was lying fallow, as well as after harvest, it was used as pasture-land by the whole village. . . . Pasture was common property, and arable land reverted from time to time to the use of the community as pasture." It is said that the Inclosure Commissioners have met with instances of arable fields which were periodically distributed by lot, each owner taking his allotment for the period of the usual rotation of the crops. "We have tried in vain (says Professor Nasse) to obtain further information concerning these very interesting conditions, which might form an instructive supplement to the *Gehöferschaften* in the district of Treves. In no place, except Mr. Blamire's statement before the Committee in 1844, either in the writings of ancient or modern authors, have we found such a system of agriculture mentioned; however frequent it may have been with regard to the meadows, it must have been very rare upon arable land." The system of allotments which prevailed in the district of Treves is described in the Reports on the Tenure of land in different countries, which were published by the Government in 1869. The peasants are there described as holding all the land in common, excepting a few private estates, and excepting houses and gardens. All the rest of the land was periodically distributed by lot, the quantity in each lot depending on the purchased or inherited rights of the allottee. The drawings for the arable land were originally held every three years, but afterwards at longer intervals. But as far as the law of property in England is concerned, there is very little evidence of a similar distribution of arable, and it is safer to hold with the latest authorities, that the village, as it first appears in our history, is in every case " either a body of free landowners who have advanced beyond the stage of land-community, or the body of tenants of a lord who regulates them, or allows them to regulate themselves on principles derived from the same source." (Stubbs, "Const. Hist." i. 85.) In any case, it is obvious enough that the co-operative husbandry, which has lasted to our own times in so many places, is the offshoot of some earlier set of institutions which recognized the local community as owning all the lands within its district.

The evils which arose in modern times from the survival of the common-field husbandry are sufficiently well known. The open farms produced hardly enough food to maintain the scanty population of the villages, and it has been seriously maintained by some authorities that the science of agriculture had in many parts steadily deteriorated from the time of Edward the Confessor to the middle of the reign of George III., when a great movement for reform began. In the year 1773 an Act was passed for the better regulation of common arable fields, wastes, and pastures, which provides that three-fourths in number and value of the owners may determine the course of management notwithstanding any local usage. It was further enacted that every severalty owner might inclose his land, even in the absence of a local custom of inclosure, and that the cottagers who had rights of common at certain seasons, without being owners of allotments, should either be duly compensated or continue to exercise the right. The benefit of these provisions will be understood when it is remembered that primitive usage determined in each village the division of the arable into two or three long fields, the rotation of crops, the erection and removal of fences, and every other detail of rustic management. In places where the custom of inclosure did not prevail, and where there was no right to change the bye-laws as occasion required, a field might become useless to its private owners, because the common flock or herd must be let in on a day too early for the removal of the crops, the forefathers of the village having never contemplated the cultivation of anything better than pulse or rye. The allotments were dispersed in little patches, each fragment in one field corresponding to others of equal size or value in the other fields belonging to the same owner, and a great part of the land was necessarily taken up with the main roads leading through the fields, and a multitude of driftways leading to the intermixed allotments. The famous Naseby Field was described by the Board of Agriculture as lying almost in a state of nature, the avenues across the field going zig-zag, as chance directed, with the hollows and sloughs unfilled except by mire. The Report of the Inclosure Committee of 1844 will furnish examples of several parishes, where areas of 2,000 acres and upwards were cut up into open pieces of the average size of three roods; and unfortunately these might have been some of the best land in the country, being the portions selected as most promising when the country was originally settled. Mr. Blamire mentioned also in his evidence, that persons called flock-masters had frequently the right of feeding their sheep over all the land in the parish, " or sometimes only on part, so that persons may have an opportunity of putting in a wheat crop," but in many places no one could sow a crop without first making a bargain with the master of the flock. Instances like this may make one understand the rough German proverb, " Gesammt Gut verdammt Gut," and they might be multiplied by evidence from every part of the country, excepting Devonshire and Cornwall, where the common-field system did not prevail. It will be sufficient to close this part of the subject with an extract from a prize-essay by an eminent authority on farming. Mr. Clare Sewell Read has stated (Royal Agric. Proc. 1854) that the greatest improvements which have taken place in Oxfordshire are those produced by inclosures:—

"The only wonder is that, the advantages being so manifest, any parish should be left uninclosed throughout the country. Persons living at a distance cannot comprehend the miseries of common-field. They could hardly credit that a parish containing 1,000 acres should be cut up into 1200 or 1300 strips, that the whole parish must be cropped on one course, and that the meadows belong to one individual from the 1st of May to the 1st of August, and are afterwards commonable to the whole of the parish. Then there is the loss by trotting from one piece of land to another, the trouble occasioned to the farmer in overlooking a small farm, the certainty of distemper, such as pleuro-pneumonia in cattle or the foot-disease in sheep, being disseminated over the whole parish if once introduced, the impossibility of draining detached half-acres, and the constant source of quarrels from trespassing and ploughing on another's land. In some open-field parishes the lands are large and the meadows not Lammas-ground. Here the benefits derivable from inclosing are not so great, yet numerous advantages would well repay the trouble and cost of an allotment."

The different kinds of open-lands, not

being manorial wastes, may be classified as follows:—

(*a.*) Arable lands, called "shack-fields," which are held in severalty during a portion of the year, until the crop has been removed, when the whole field becomes commonable to the cattle of the severalty owners, but not to those of other persons.

(*b.*) There are some few instances, says Mr. Wingrove Cooke, in which arable land is found with all the incidents of a common-field, except that there is no right of intercommoning upon the stubbles.

(*c.*) Lammas lands, so called from Old Lammas Day, when harvest thanksgivings were celebrated and the commons usually thrown open to all the cattle of the village. These are described as arable fields or meadows, held in separate ownership for some months in the year and inclosed with movable fences, or with stones and boundary lines, which are commonable when the crops have been removed, not only to the separate owners but also to a larger body of commoners, such as all the tenants of the manor or all the owners and occupiers in the parish. The day of removing the fences was the occasion of an annual merry-making, of which the tradition has survived in many places, and where the portions of the separate owners were distributed by lot, the day when the common pasturage reverted to private ownership was made in like manner the occasion for another procession or feast. The shifting ownerships and lot-meadows, which are found in several districts among the Lammas lands, will presently be described.

(d.) In the next place come " stinted pastures" of various kinds, which all fall under the description of grazing-land, where the owners of the soil or some other class of persons have rights of pasturage for a limited number of cattle. The limited rights are known as cattle-gates or stints, and in almost every county have some local name—such as a cows-grass, a sheep-leaze, or a beast-gate. And it depends upon minute points respecting the title to the soil apart from the herbage, whether the persons with grazing rights are to be treated as commoners or as partners in a landed estate. When the freemen of a borough have rights over the corporation-fields, it will usually be found that their interests represent shares in a stinted pasture, rather than rights of common in the ordinary sense of the term.

(e.) In some parts of the country there are large tracts of commonable wood-land where commoners can turn in stock at any time of year: so that the owner of the woods has no means of preserving his property. But it should be remembered that by the Inclosure Act, 29 Geo. II. c. 36, the assent of a majority of the commoners may authorize the temporary inclosure of wastes and commonable lands for the better growth and preservation of trees. And by various private Acts and local customs the owners of a commonable wood may inclose against the commoners' cattle. In one case, for instance, the tenants of a manor in Gloucestershire were shown to have " the herbage, &c., of the common woods, and common hills, and the lord's waste, saving that the lord for the time being, for the better breeding and increase of wood, may inclose one full third part of all the woods and wood-grounds of the manor."

And there are several other varieties of commonable land, such as dole-moors and sheep-walks in mountainous districts, where the surface and the soil are not unfrequently in different ownerships, and other kinds, which need not be now described.

But, before leaving this part of the subject, it seems worth while to describe the shifting severalties, or "moveable fee-simples," which still remain in certain country districts, to the confusion of all who have to deal with their owners. It is not long since a great railway company got into trouble for neglecting to treat the owner of one of these wandering properties with the respect which is due to those whose land is taken for the public benefit.

It appears from the Report of 1844 that there is great variety in the holdings upon these commonable lands. In some places they have what is called a pane of land, in which there may be forty or sixty lots. "It often happens that in these shifting severalties the occupier of wot 1 this year goes round the whole of the several lots in rotation: the owner of Lot 1 this year has Lot 2 next year, and so on: arable lands change not annually but periodically, according to the rotation of the crops." This is curiously similar to the Irish system of "run-dale holdings," which Sir H. Maine has described in his latest work as a system under which a definite area is occupied by a group of families, the arable being held in severalty and the bog and pasture in common. But so lately (he says) as fifty years since, cases were frequent in which the arable land was divided into farms which shifted among the tenant-families periodically, and sometimes annually.

The lot-meadows are managed somewhat differently. The meadow, or the dole-moor or fen, as the case might be, was divided into lots each bearing a special mark, such as a horn, a hand-reel, four oxen and a horse, or the like: and it may deserve notice, that in many parts of the country the names of the fields, as Bird-and-Bush Shot, Old-man Shot and the like, testify to the prevalence of tenure by lot in former times. Then on a certain day in every year the proprietors or their tenants assembled and drew lots for portions, the customary marks being cut on apples or pieces of wood which were drawn at random from a bag. Probably the best account of a lot-meadow is to be found in Giles's "History of Bampton," where a hamlet is described which from the most ancient times has been managed in all matters relating to the open fields and commons by four officers called Grass-stewards and sixteen representatives of the land-owners called the Sixteens. After giving a minute account of the arable farming, the narrator describes the cumbersome machinery by which the villagers divided their pasture-lands:—

"The common meadow is laid out by boundary stones into thirteen large divisions technically called layings-out; these always remain the same, and each is divided into four sets. As the meadow is not equally fertile in every part, it is desirable to adopt some mode of giving all an equal chance of obtaining the best cuts for their cattle. From time immemorial there have been sixteen marks established in the village, each of which corresponds with four yard-lands (allotments in the lands of the village). A certain number of the tenants consequently have the same mark, which they always keep, the use of these marks enabling the tenants every year to draw lots for their portions of the meadow. When the grass is fit to cut, the grass stewards and sixteens summon the tenants to a general meeting, and the following ceremony takes place. Four of the tenants come forward, each bearing his mark cut on a piece of wood,—as the frying-pan, the hern's foot, &c. The first drawn entitles its owner to have his portion in Set 1, the second in Set 2, and so on; and thus four tenants having obtained their allotments, four others come forward, and the process is repeated. When the lots are all drawn, each man cuts out his mark upon his piece of ground, which in many cases is so narrow a strip that he has not width enough for a full sweep of the scythe . . . and another peculiarity of the system is that a single farmer may have to cut his portion of the grass from twenty different places."

Chapter III.

INCLOSURES.

Disputes as to commons and wastes.—Approvement.—Early inclosures. — Statute of Merton. — Open spaces Committee.—Means of securing public recreation ground.—Disputes as to common fields.—Changes in system of agriculture.—Effect of inclosures and changing arable to pasture.—Rebellions. — Local Inclosure Acts.— Lord Worsley's Act.—Open spaces round London.—Early complaints of growth of London.—Decay of archery.—Riots.—Proclamations against building.—The Metropolitan Commons Acts.—Memorandum of Inclosure Commissioners.

THERE are three long-standing disputes regarding waste lands and open fields which are now, as we hope, to be peaceably composed. For the quarrel which once blazed out in civil war, when Ket the Tanner sat under the Oak of Reformation, and Protector Somerset lost his head, has degenerated into a tiresome wrangle about the compensation to be paid for public play-grounds, which the new Inclosure Act, *pulveris exigui jactu*, will possibly bring to an end.

These disputes concerned the approvement of wastes, the inclosure of common fields, and the increase of building round London.

When the greater part of England was occupied by moors and fens, the process of inclosure was looked at with no disfavour, and long before the Statute of Merton was passed, it seems that many large improvements had been made. Richard of Deeping obtained leave from the Abbot of Croyland to inclose and drain a great portion of the common marsh: "he made a large town and very fertile fields, and out of a horrible fen he made a garden of delight." "In imitation of this spirited cultivator," says Mr. Hallam, "the inhabitants of Spalding and some neighbouring villages divided their marshes among them, when some converting them to tillage, others reserving them for meadow or leaving them in pasture, they found a rich soil for every purpose, and many villages and the Abbey itself followed their example. This early instance of parochial inclosure is not to be overlooked in the history of social progress."

Then came the Statute of Merton, said to be a declaration of the common law, providing that lords of manors might inclose their waste lands as against their tenants who had rights of pasture there, upon proof that sufficient remained for the use of the commoner's cattle. As no one besides tenants was mentioned, it was soon found that the commoners from adjoining districts were likely to raise a perpetual opposition to these inclosures, and it was therefore enacted by the Second Statute of Westminster, that "whereas in the Statute of Merton it was provided and granted that owners of wastes might inclose the same, notwithstanding the opposition of their tenants, so that those tenants had sufficient pasture for their holdings, with free ingress and egress for cattle, and because no mention was made of inclosures between neighbours, many owners of wastes have been hindered from inclosing by the opposition of neighbours who had pasture enough; and whereas the tenants of a stranger have no more right than a man's own tenants to feed cattle on his waste, therefore the said Statute of Merton should thenceforth be enforced between neighbours as well as between a lord and his tenants." And after the rebellions in the reign of Edward VI., both Statutes were confirmed and in some respects extended.

These Acts, however, apply only to the ordinary rights of pasture, and if a commoner has privileges of taking peat, or wood, or fish, &c., a private inclosure will not be allowed to interfere with his rights. The owners are not prevented from inclosing by the fact that some person has a power of taking gravel in another part of the common: nor will the commoner be in danger of losing his profits because the people interested in the herbage have arranged to make an inclosure. The Open Spaces Committee of 1865 advised very strongly that the Statute of Merton should be repealed, as having fulfilled its purpose and being superseded by modern legislation, and as being especially ill-adapted to commons and open spaces near the metropolis: and other proposals have often been made to the same effect, including plans for getting rid of inconvenient claims by declaratory Acts and the like, which show more reverence for legal forms than for the principles on which the law has hitherto been administered. All parties are agreed, in fact, that proper recreation ground must be secured to the public, but there is great opposition to any comprehensive scheme of purchase. Putting aside all questions as to commons in the metropolitan area, and taking the case of an open space which it is desired to retain for the public enjoyment, it would seem that only three courses are available to the authorities who may be concerned in the matter: they can buy the land, or take it without buying it, or wait to see what the proprietors wish to do. If there are many persons interested in the property, it is very likely that they may never agree to do anything; but if there are few, say three owners of an open arable field, or the lord of a manor with five copyholders having the only rights of pasture, or if there should be a hundred owners who have all agreed to inclose, then surely it would be expedient that some public officer should have powers of compulsory purchase. And in fact, the Committee of 1865, in the case of the metropolitan commoners, recommended that similar powers should be provided, "if in any case it be possible to acquire the rights of the lord or of the commoners for the benefit of the public, as affording a greater security against any possible inclosure." Nor can it be supposed that there would be more difficulty in estimating and apportioning the price, than is found in dividing the compensation paid by a railway company, between a lord and commoners or a body of joint proprietors.

The inclosure of the common fields led at one time to fiercer disputes than were ever caused by the Statute of Merton. Before the sixteenth century the fields were almost all in tillage, and cattle-breeding upon artificial pastures was unknown or altogether neglected. Land was very cheap, and the landlords were glad to let their demesnes upon lives, or from year to year, at very trifling rents. But soon after the discovery of America, and the consequent flow of gold and silver to Europe, a remarkable change took place in English agriculture, which caused a hundred years of bickering and rebellion, and which even now is often described as an organized scheme of robbery by which the rich got possession of the lands of the poor. The discovery was made that landed property might become exceedingly valuable if a more scientific plan of farming were introduced. The high prices offered for hides and wool upon the Continent indicated the source of future profit, and the natural results followed upon the discovery. Landlords turned their attention at once to mixed husbandry with a rude rotation of grass and grain: and they at once inclosed their farms and their share of the village fields, as a necessary step towards the introduction of the new husbandry. But the radical feature of the change was not so much the inclosure of open land, as the introduction upon tracts of ancient arable of a course of mixed farming, better adapted to the climate of most of the counties and to the demands of the foreign market. And it is one of the chief merits of Professor Nasse's account of our mediæval agriculture, that he pointed out the true character of these events and the necessity, when the change had once commenced, that the old system should be completely superseded by methods of agriculture more suited to the capabilities of the soil. He considers it probable that the plan of a permanent separation of pasture land "was imported by a people whose former place of residence had a continental climate, and we may presume that these were the Anglo-Saxons: the movement of the sixteenth century was a return to the state of agriculture naturally suited to England." But the first results of the change were alarming in the highest degree. The statutes of that time are filled with complaints of the depopulation of villages and the general diminution of tillage: "many houses and villages are deserted, and the arable land belonging to them is inclosed and converted into pasture: and where formerly two hundred men supported themselves by honest labour, only two or three shepherds are now to be seen." It was said of Thorpe in Nottinghamshire, that the inclosures had so ruined the place "that there was not a house left inhabited in this notable lordship, but a shepherd only kept ale to sell in the church." After the suppression of the monasteries the new proprietors of the abbey-lands pursued the same system of inclosure and conversion of arable into pasture, which occasioned more complaints and murmurs from the people. "Nay," says the historian, "several little books were published showing the mischief of these proceedings, but the nobility and gentry still pursued the same course, without regarding the consequences. It happened in 1548, that the Lords passed a bill for giving everyone leave to inclose his ground if he pleased: but the bill was thrown out by the Commons, and yet the lords and gentlemen went on inclosing their lands." One result of all this was a rebellion in every part of the country; but a more permanent evil was the spread of a mischievous belief that private property in land was only another name for the robbery of the people. In an old appeal to Parliament we find the doctrine thus expressed:

"He that sells the earth and he that buys do remove the landmark from the third person, and they two that buy and sell and leave the land for an inheritance to their children, they murder the third man, because they steal away his livelihood. For after a man has bought the land and paid the money, he saith: 'This is my land, I have paid for it.' But the third man comes in and saith: 'The land is mine, equal with you by the law of creation:' and so the buyer he begins to draw his sword and to fight, and if he conquer he rejoices and saith: 'This land is now mine indeed: I have bought and I have conquered.' But, thou covetous person, so long as there is another man besides thee and him whom thou hast killed, the earth belongs to him as well as to thee. Therefore now the common people have more true title to the common land than lords of manors have, yet we shut them not out, but let them take part with us, as fellow creatures."

From the time of the civil war to the passing of the General Act of 1773, very little was done towards the regulation or inclosure of the common fields which remained, but after that time a great number of local Acts were passed for the inclosure of commonable lands and wastes, and the confirmation of agreements to inclose made between owners and commoners, where legal difficulties made it impossible to get the concurrence of all the persons interested.

In 1836 the general measure, known as Lord Worsley's Act, was passed to facilitate inclosures in common fields; but its provisions have in practice been superseded by the more convenient procedure of the Inclosure Commission. This Act does not apply to manorial wastes or any waste land where one person owns the soil and others have rights of taking the produce; but a great number of inclosures are said to have been made under colour of its provisions, to which the machinery of the statute was not intended to apply. Nor does it extend to open fields or pastures in the immediate neighbourhood of London or other large cities and towns, and it has been justly remarked, that the clause which imposes this restriction was the first indication that public policy might in some cases be opposed to the inclosure of commons. But with these exceptions the Act permits the inclosure of open arable fields, meadows, and pastures which are held in severalty for a portion of the year, by commissioners appointed with the consent of two-thirds in number and value of the persons interested, or if seven-eighths of the number consent, without the intervention of commissioners.

Little need be said here of the history of the third dispute. The old chroniclers are full of laments over the increased bulk of London and the destruction of suburban fields. When the practice of archery began to languish, many reasons were advanced to account for the change in the national habit, and it grew to be a common belief that archery would have continued to flourish if it had not been for the over-rapid inclosures. "Why should I speak of archery," says Stow, "when by means of inclosing of common grounds our men, for want of room to shoot abroad, creep into bowling allies and ordinary dicing houses?" And he cites the description of a riot from a much older writer, which reads almost as fresh as if it had happened yesterday. "The inhabitants of the towns about London, such as Islington and Shoreditch, had so inclosed their common fields that neither the young men of the city might shoot, nor the ancient persons walk for their pleasure in those fields, but either their bows and arrows were broken, or those honest persons were arrested or indicted, saying that no Londoner ought to go out of the city but by the highways. This saying so grieved the Londoners, that a great number assembled, and a turner in a fool's coat came crying through the city, 'Shovels and spades! shovels and spades!' So many of the people followed that it was a wonder to behold, and within a short space all the hedges about the city were cast down, such was the diligence of those workmen."

King James I. was fond of archers, and morbidly afraid of the overgrowth of London, and in many proclamations he endeavoured to stay the plague of inclosures and increase of building. He ordained that no archers' butts should be removed from any field, and that no impediment to archery should be permitted within two miles of London or Westminster. Commissioners were sent to pull down all new buildings within that limit, and to level all hedges of an inconvenient height. In the next reign the Lord Mayor was sent upon a similar commission, but from that time we hear very little of the matter, except Stow's lamentations over the inclosures at Shoreditch and the buildings in Ratcliffe Highway. But in the reign of George III. a cowkeeper named Pitfield pulled down one of the ancient butts in Finsbury Fields, and was compelled to rebuild it by the Artillery Company under the obsolete powers of the Commission of 1632: and it is said that the words " Pitfield's repentance " were for many years to be seen carved on the butt in memory of the victory of the citizens. But afterwards came a dark period of inclosing and building, filling all the commons with streets and squares, until the recent Acts prevented their extension into any of the wastes and common fields remaining in the metropolitan district; and if more open spaces are required, the Acts can doubtless be extended to other lands in the district.

The Inclosure Commissioners have recently issued an important memorandum, describing the course of modern legislation with reference to the inclosure of commons, and this it will be best to adopt as the official history of the matter. But it will be remembered that inclosures can be made in a great variety of instances without coming within the jurisdiction of the Commissioners; as by the Statute of Merton and the Acts which extended its operation, or by agreement of all persons interested, or by a custom authorizing the lord of a manor to inclose with the consent of a jury of commoners, or by the usage of inclosure among severalty owners in a common field, or the usage of tenants to take in portions of a waste for raising a crop of wheat, and so on in a great number of instances under the authority of Acts of Parliament, customs, and usages applying to particular districts.

The modern history of inclosures and the principles which are embodied in the Bill which is now before Parliament will appear very clearly from the following extracts from the published Memorandum:—

"Up to 1845 inclosures were only made under private Bills. In 1801 was passed an Inclosure Clauses Consolidation Act to be incorporated with any private Inclosure Bill. It was designed not to benefit lords of the manor, but with a view exclusively to the public interest. It was prompted partly by the exigencies of the French war and partly by the desire to maintain a system of protection, and had for its special object to secure the increase of home-grown grain in order to render Great Britain independent of foreign countries for its food supply.

"The present General Inclosure Act was passed in 1845. The procedure which it introduced was that of Provisional Order. The Inclosure Commissioners make a Provisional Order, approving an inclosure scheme made in conformity with the provisions of the General Inclosure Act; then they move the Home Secretary to bring in a confirming Bill to confirm this Order, and when the Bill is passed carry out the inclosure in manner prescribed by the General Inclosure Act. After 1845, for many years, there was every year an annual Inclosure Bill to confirm the several schemes that had been approved by the Commissioners during the previous year.

"The office of the Secretary of State in bringing in this confirming Bill was always looked upon as purely ministerial. He did not revise the work of the Commissioners, and until recently Parliament was accustomed to pass the Bill without question. Practically, the matter was exclusively in the hands of the Commissioners, subject only to the provisions of the General Inclosure Act.

"That Act, like the Act of 1801, was intended to facilitate inclosure for the sake of agricultural improvement; it did not recognize (no Act or legal decision has ever recognized) any right in the public at large over commons; but it contained many provisions in behalf of the public, provisions such as it seemed equitable to impose upon landowners seeking from the Legislature additional facilities in order to give effect to their rights in a manner likely to be prejudicial to the enjoyments of the local community. For instance, the Commissioners were expressly required, before making a provisional order, to have regard to the health, comfort, and convenience of the inhabitants of any cities, towns, villages, or populous places, in or near any parish or place where the land proposed to be inclosed, or any part thereof, was situate. Again, in case the inclosure related to lands within a prescribed distance of towns having a prescribed population, the Commissioners were required to state, in their provisional order, the special grounds on which they were of opinion that the inclosure was expedient.

"In order also to modify the effects of inclosure the Act provided for two kinds of public allotments—allotments for exercise and recreation, and allotments of field gardens for the labouring poor, the former being left to the discretion of the Commissioners, the latter being made obligatory.

"But of late years various considerations have combined to produce a widespread feeling, both in and out of Parliament, in favour of a revision of the Inclosure Laws. The principal of these seem to be the following:—

"1. Circumstances have materially changed since the passing of the Act of 1801, and even since 1845. The special object of the first Act —to make Great Britain independent of foreign countries for its food supply—may be said to have ceased to exist under a system of peace and free trade. On the other hand, the increase of the town population during the last three quarters of a century, and the great number and extent of inclosures made during the same period, seem in the eyes of many to render it as much the interest of the public that open spaces should be kept open as that waste lands should be brought into cultivation.

"2. The immediate object of the original Inclosure Acts—viz., to facilitate inclosures for agricultural purposes, has been by no means always attained. The Act equally facilitates inclosures for any other purpose, since as soon as the allotments are acquired in severalty the owners can appropriate them to any purpose they please,—for instance, to building or to the preservation of game, or planting.

"3. The provisions of the Inclosure Acts for the protection of the community have been suffered to become to a great extent inoperative. Until very recently it was the acknowledged practice of the Commissioners to look on inclosures as private improvements, and to recommend any inclosure that was proposed to them, provided that the parties having proprietary rights desired it.

"In 1865 a Select Committee was appointed to consider the subject of open spaces near the metropolis. This led to the passing, in the following year, of the Metropolitan Commons Act. The effect of that Act was to exclude the Metropolitan Police District from the operation of the Inclosure Commissioners, and in consequence to disable lords of manors, within those limits, from inclosing, except—1, By a private Bill; or 2, by approving under the statute of Merton; or 3, by obtaining the sanction of all the commoners. The same Act provided for the making of schemes for the local management of metropolitan commons.

"In 1869 a Select Committee was appointed to consider the General Inclosure Act, especially with reference to its effect on the labouring poor. The committee made numerous recommendations with a view to secure for the future that there should be a more liberal assignment of public allotments, and that fuller information should be laid before Parliament with respect to each proposed inclosure. The committee also expressed their opinion that no further inclosure should be allowed until such of their recommendations as Parliament might approve should have been incorporated with the existing Acts.

"The proposals of the Select Committee of 1869 were briefly as follows:—

"1. A more satisfactory conduct of the preliminary inquiry by the Assistant Commissioner.

"2. A more precise and complete report of the Inclosure Commissioners to Parliament.

"3. As to recreation allotments, abolition of statutory *maximum*.

"4. As to garden allotments:—(a) Power to assign allotment up to half-an-acre; (b) expense of clearing to be deemed part of expenses of enclosure.

"5. As to both kinds of allotments:—(a) Facilities of exchange with a view to procure eligible sites; (b) appropriation of surplus rents to similar objects; (c) better management.

"6. Power to set out paths and roads. With respect to the proposal of the Select Committee of 1871 to submit inclosure schemes to a Select Committee to be annually appointed, reference may be made to the practice which during the last few years has been followed with great success in the case of turnpike trusts.

"A similar course might be adopted with advantage in the case of inclosures. The inclosures recommended by the Commissioners would be referred, at the commencement of the session, to a Select Committee, and it would only be on the recommendation of that committee that the Secretary of State would bring in an Inclosure Bill.

"There remains the further question whether the principle of the Metropolitan Commons Act should be extended to suburbs of towns in the provinces. If a *locus standi* before the Commissioners were expressly granted to urban sanitary authorities, it would be sufficient to rely upon the power of the Select Committee either to reject any proposal for a suburban inclosure which seemed inexpedient, or to substitute for inclosure a scheme of regulated pastures. It does not seem advisable to give to local authorities the power of a veto upon proposed inclosures."

Chapter IV.

PROVISIONS OF THE BILL.

Objects of Bill.—Method of procedure.—What lands are included.—Definitions.—Applications to Commissioners.—Who are persons interested.—Consents, how to be given.—Compensation on inclosure.—Saving of manorial rights, whether required.—Customary rights of miners, whether to be protected.—Regulation of Commons by General Inclosure Act.—New provisions.—Improvement of Commons.—Old powers of improvement, whether to be abolished.—Regulation of Commons which do not come under the Act.—Estates and interests of owners and commoners.—Whether they can be acquired for the public benefit.—What provisions would be necessary.

THERE are some points, relating to the scope and efficacy of the measure now proposed, which require the attention of all who are beneficially interested in wastes and commonable fields. The Act is not merely intended to throw difficulties in the way of inclosing wild heaths and moors, but may be applied to the permanent regulation of any wastes or commonable fields, with special reference to the needs of the neighbouring population, so that with certain consents half the farms in a parish may be converted into a public garden for the nearest town.

The same procedure is to be used for the inclosure and the permanent regulation of commons, which are objects of a very opposite nature; and it is probable that some difficulty will be found in applying to the formation of agreeable recreation grounds the machinery which was framed to facilitate private partitions.

The Act is to extend to all lands which are subject to be inclosed under the Inclosure Acts, 1845 to 1868, except Metropolitan commons, which are defined as "commons" within the meaning of the 11th section of the Act of 1845, the whole or any part of which is situate within the Metropolitan Police District.

The various kinds of land which can be inclosed under these Acts have already been described, but it may still be useful to quote the official description of the lands which are to be regulated or inclosed under the measure which is now proposed. In the Act of 1845 these lands are described as follows:—

(*a.*) "All lands subject to any rights of common whatsoever, and whether such rights may be exercised and enjoyed at all times, or only during limited times, seasons, or periods, or may be subject to any suspension or restriction in respect of the time of the enjoyment thereof":

(*b.*) "All gated and stinted pastures, in which the property of the soil or part thereof is in the owners of the cattle-gates or other gates or stints or any of them: also all gated or stinted pastures, in which no part of the property of the soil is in the owners of the cattle-gates, &c."

(*c.*) "All lands held or occupied or used in common, either at all times or during any time or season or periodically, and either for all purposes or for any limited purpose, and whether the separate parcels of the several owners of the soil shall or shall not be known by metes or bounds or be otherwise distinguishable":

(*d.*) " All land in which the property or right of or to the vesture or herbage, or any part thereof, during the whole or any part of the year, or of or to the wood or underwood growing and to grow thereon, is separated from the ownership of the soil:"

(*e.*) " All lot-meadows and other lands, where the occupation or enjoyment of the separate lots or parcels is subject to interchange among the respective owners in any known course of rotation or otherwise ".

By the Act of 1848 any lands, not otherwise the subject of a pending inclosure, may be brought under its operation upon terms to be approved by the Commissioners; and by the Act of 1854, the word "land" is extended to incorporeal hereditaments. All lands in the New Forest and the Forest of Dean, are exempted from inclosure under the Acts.

Definitions.

It is not very clear whether the legal terms used in the Bill are to be taken in the sense given to such terms by the Act of 1845. But in any case it seems desirable to provide that the Act shall apply to lands of every tenure, to prevent disputes as to whether copyholds are included in its operation. General Acts do not apply to copyholds, unless they are expressly mentioned, where any prejudice may accrue to a lord or tenant by reason of the alteration of interest, tenure, or custom: thus, for instance, the exchange provisions of the Act of 1845 had to be extended to copyholds in express words by the Act of 1846. In the same way it is desirable to provide, in express terms, for the case of any local customs which it is intended to affect by the words of a general Act. The word "manor" should extend to all manors or lordships, or reputed manors or lordships, because the reputation that a legal manor has existed is sufficient title to the soil of a waste without proof of the holding of courts, or of the existence of at least two freehold tenancies. The words "commoners," and "rights of common," should extend to the interests of persons who have "stinted rights" in the herbage or produce of commons without being commoners in the strict sense of the term.

The expression "waste land of a manor" is defined in sect. 28, as meaning and including any land which consists (1) of waste of a manor where the tenants have rights of common, (2) of land subject to rights of common for cattle *levant* and *couchant* at all times in the year, or in other words, land subject to be grazed at all seasons by as many cattle as the commoner's land can sustain, and (3) of land subject to any rights of common which may be exercised at all times in the year, and which are not limited by number or stints, unless the context otherwise requires. The description is borrowed from the Act of 1845, where it is applied to lands which are not to be inclosed without giving allotments to the neighbouring inhabitants. The language of the definition seems to relate exclusively to rights of pasture, and not to apply to wastes where the commoners have only rights of taking fuel, gravel, and the like. There are many wastes of manors where the tenants' grazing rights are stinted under customary bye-laws, or under the provisions of a public or local Act of Parliament, but as the Bill stands the word "waste" is used in a restricted artificial sense for lands where the cattle, which the commoners' land can sustain, may be fed at all times of the year without stint, and all other wastes are included with commonable fields and woods in the description of "commons which are not wastes of manors."

Applications relating to Commons.

The Commissioners are allowed by sect. 2 to entertain applications for the regulation or inclosure of a common, or the regulation of part and the inclosure of the residue of a common, but are not to carry such application into effect before they are satisfied that the applicants represent one-third in value of the interests affected; and by sect. 12 they must also be satisfied, before certifying the expediency of a provisional order, that persons representing at least two-thirds in value of such interests as are affected have given their consent. It would seem to be necessary to insert some definition of persons interested, either in express words or by reference to the Acts of 1845 and 1852. Persons interested within the meaning of those Acts, are defined to be the persons answering to the following description, and no others, viz.: the persons in possession of the land or right of common, including lessees under long terms of years in certain cases, but excluding all who have a less estate than a lease for life, at a rent exceeding two-thirds of the value, the persons next in remainder to such excepted persons being treated as the persons in possession; but the excepted persons are entitled to vote in matters relating to inclosure jointly with the persons in possession, and there are similar provisions for giving joint-votes to receivers and creditors in possession. Other provisions are made for cases where the Crown, the Duchy of Lancaster, or the Duchy of Cornwall may be interested in an inclosure; and for giving joint votes to joint-tenants, coparceners, and tenants in common: and in cases of disability the guardian, trustee, committee, &c., or in default any person nominated by the Commissioners, are, for the purposes of the Acts, to be substituted for the persons interested. These provisions are appropriate to the case of an inclosure, where the only object is to exchange an interest in the uninclosed common for an allotment to be held under a precisely similar title. But how can these provisions be applied in practice to the regulation of common with a general adjustment of rights, and a prohibition of inclosure in the future? Is a tenant for life, or a trustee, or husband, or guardian, or a person to be named by the Commissioners, to be enabled to give up all control over the property without being assured of an equivalent, or if they are so enabled, would persons in a fiduciary position be advised to take the responsibility? But the difficulty will not arise if proper compensation is provided for the diminution which may be caused in the value of the property, with an appeal from the Commissioners' decision in doubtful cases.

Where the freemen, burgesses, or inhabitant householders of any city, borough, or town are entitled to rights of common or other interest in the common, the consent must be obtained of two-thirds in number of such of the freemen and burgesses so entitled as may be resident in the city, borough, or town, or within seven miles thereof, or of such inhabitant householders as the case may be (s. 12, subs. 6). This provision is taken from the Act of 1845, s. 27. By the Act of 1848, s. 1, it is provided that an order for inclosure may set forth any special agreement or matter concerning the lands to be inclosed, and Mr. Wingrove Cooke states that under this clause an agreement might be introduced to the effect that the lands where such freemen, &c., have rights shall never be inclosed, but shall be used perpetually as a regulated pasture. " The power thus limited may be found useful to regulate without inclosing some of the open commons near large towns, to the inclosure of which well-founded objections would occur." It may be worth remarking that these rights of freemen, &c., are confined to those who can show their title within the ancient district to which the right was originally limited: and that the enlargement of a borough under a modern Act of Parliament would not confer any right of sharing in the common upon the new class of residents. But a provisional order under the new Act is to give the Commissioners power in such cases (s. 4. subs. 3) to determine the persons by whom such rights are to be exercised.

When the common to which the order relates is "waste of a manor," or land within any manor to the soil of which the lord is entitled in right of his manor, then the person interested, or his substitute under the provisions of the Act of 1845 which have already been mentioned (including a substitute nominated by the Commissioners in default of the trustees, guardians, &c. of a person under disability), must consent to the order; and where there are several interested persons the Commissioners are not to report the expediency of the order, in case such persons, or the majority in respect of interest, signify their dissent within a time to be fixed by the Commissioners (s. 12, subs. 6, and Act of 1845, ss. 27, 29; Act of 1852, s. 1).

The last is obviously a very dangerous clause as regards fiduciary owners and persons under disability; but with regard to this clause, and all the other provisions respecting the protection of private interests, it must be remembered that "regard is to be had to private interests" (Preamble), and that every provisional order is to be made in a manner consistent with law (s. 12).

Compensation on Inclosure.

Very little is said in the Bill upon this subject, but by s. 6, an order for inclosure means an order for inclosing a common as provided by the Inclosure Acts, 1845 to 1868, "as amended by this Act," and the marginal note defines "inclosure" as an inclosure in manner provided by the Inclosure Acts. Taking these statements in connection with s. 12 of the Bill, it may be assumed that an inclosure order will direct the division of the common among the claimants in proportion to their interests, provided the claims have been delivered in writing and otherwise as the Acts direct, and subject to the provisions for the benefit of the neighbourhood which the Commissioners are to be authorised to insert in the order. (Ss. 7, 12.)

The allotment to the lord of the manor may consist of an allotment or a rent-charge (Act of 1845, s. 76; Act of 1846, s. 5). Where the lord is entitled to the minerals as part of the soil, his rights may be reserved, and easements for working and rights of entry and working powers given to him, subject to payment of compensation for surface damage: and where the lord or any other person owns the minerals as a property distinct from the ownership of the surface, the right to the minerals is not to be in any way affected by the inclosure, unless compensation is awarded. And under the Act of 1848, s. 1, rights of sporting, and of taking brick-earth, which is not treated as a mineral under these Acts, and rights of other kinds, may be reserved by an agreement embodied in the provisional order.

With respect to these private interests it is now proposed (s. 12) that in every provisional order for regulating or inclosing a common a statement shall be contained showing—

1. Where the interest of any lord of the manor in the soil of a common or in mineral or other rights may be affected by the order, the allotment (if any) or other compensation to be allotted or made to the lord in respect of his interest so affected:

2. Where any minerals or other rights in relation thereto belong to persons other than the lord, which may be affected by

the order, showing such provisions and reservations as are required to be inserted by the Inclosure Acts, or as may appear to the Commissioners proper to be inserted :

3. If there are any other rights which appear to the Commissioners proper to be specially provided for or to be excepted from the operation of the order, the provisions or exceptions are to be specified.

The whole matter, in short, is to be left to the direction of the Commissioners, who are to pay due regard to private interests and act according to law ; but it may be noticed that the lord's interests in the minerals, whether claimed as part of the soil or as a separate property from the ownership of the surface, are intended apparently to be extinguished, and compensation given by an allotment, rent-charge, or otherwise ; while the mineral rights of every other person are intended apparently to be continued with fresh easements and working powers, or such powers as the Commissioners may deem sufficient. The section may be intended only to mark the difference in procedure when the lord or any other persons claim the minerals as part of the soil, and when such minerals are claimed by the lord or any other persons as a property apart from the surface; but the meaning is not clear as it stands.

Before leaving this part of the subject, it may be suggested that the provisional orders for regulating and inclosing commons should contain a saving clause of the kind provided in the Act of 1845, s. 96, with suitable modifications to meet the case of regulated commons. It is thereby provided "that in every case all seigniories, royalties, franchises, and manorial jurisdictions whatsoever in or upon the land (the land to be inclosed) shall not be deemed to be compensated or extinguished, but shall be saved and excepted out of the operation of this Act, unless in and by the award it shall be declared, with the consent of the lord or respective lords interested therein, that such seigniories, franchises, royalties, and jurisdictions, shall be extinguished upon the proposed inclosure."

And it may be worth considering whether the Commissioners should be directed to provide for or except the customary or statutory rights of tin-bounders and free-miners working for minerals in such parts of Cornwall, Devon, Somerset, and Derbyshire as are affected by such rights, or whether the rights of the miners should be expressly saved by the Act.

Regulation of Commons.

There are several provisions in the Inclosure Acts (Act of 1845, ss. 113-122) enabling the Commissioners to convert the whole or part of a common into regulated pastures, to be stocked in common by the persons interested therein, in proportion to their respective rights and interests, as determined on the examination of claims; and the stints or rights of pasturage are to be in every case determined in proportion to the value of the respective rights and interests of the persons interested therein, provision being made for the equalizing of values in certain cases by the payment of small sums of money. The right of the soil of such regulated pastures, subject to the lord's rights to minerals, stone, and other substrata, and any other rights reserved to him by the Commissioners, is to be vested in the owners of the rights of pasture in proportion to the value of their respective stints. And there are various rules for the appointment of field-reeves, and for the holding of annual meetings for regulating the pasture, and for the rateable increase or diminution of the rights of pasture according to the condition of the herbage. But in the clauses of the present Bill which relate to the regulation of commons the interests of the respective owners are by no means so carefully protected.

The order for the regulation of a common may provide (s. 3) for the adjustment of rights in respect of the common or for its improvement, or for either of those purposes.

This adjustment of rights may comprise all or any of the matters following, viz.:—

1. Upon the waste of a manor, the deter-

mination of the persons by whom, the stock by which, and the times when common of pasture is to be exercised. It is not likely that this clause as it stands would enable the Commissioners to deprive anyone of his legal right of pasture. It probably means that the Commissioners are to ascertain the persons so entitled and make bye-laws for the mode in which the rights are to be used. But there is no machinery for ascertaining the persons who may be entitled, except the rules as to public meetings and personal inquiries to be conducted by the Assistant Commissioner (s. 11). The insertion of a clause is required, enacting that all claims shall be barred unless made in writing before a certain day after the holding of the public meeting, the Commissioners being given a power of receiving claims at any time before the confirmation of the order upon all costs and expenses being paid by the dilatory claimant (Act of 1845, s. 47). And where any claims are to be ascertained by the Commissioners in the course of their inquiries, it is, of course, requisite that a person aggrieved by their determination should have the right of appealing to a legal tribunal.

2. Upon the waste of a manor, the determination in the same way, as to common of turbary, or taking of estovers, or taking gravel, or otherwise interfering with the soil, of the persons by whom such rights are to be exercised, and of the mode and time of user—no provision, however, being made for a binding determination of the matter—and where all or any such rights may permanently injure the common, the adjustment of rights may comprise the restriction, modification, or abolition of any such rights, compensation being made to aggrieved persons in money, with their consent, or by the grant of a right of equal value. It does not appear very clearly how the measure of value is to be ascertained, or out of whose estate the valuable right is to be granted; but we may perhaps assume that the Commissioners are to grant a right of pasture or some other privilege in the same common, and in that case it should

be provided that no commoner should have the value of his rights decreased by the admission of another class of commoners, unless it is shown that he receives some benefit by the arrangement.

3. Upon land which is not waste of a manor, the adjustment of rights may include the stinting or other determination of the commoners' rights, and the persons by whom, and the mode in which, and the times when such rights are to be exercised; and it is to be observed that in this clause the determination of rights seems to mean more than ascertaining of the persons entitled, and to enable the Commissioners to limit the number of commoners: and where all or any such rights may be injurious to the general body of commoners or to the proper cultivation of the land, the adjustment of rights may include the abolition, restriction, or modification of such rights on compensation being made to any person aggrieved either in money, with his consent, or by the grant of a right of equal value. This clause applies to all common-

able fields and woods, and stinted pastures, and also seems to apply to manorial wastes where the pasturage is limited by stints or numbers.

4. Upon commons of every kind, the adjustment of rights may include the determination of the rights and obligations of the lord of the manor, severalty owners, or other persons entitled to the soil, which are matters which cannot be determined without a limitation of the time for making claims, and an appeal in doubtful cases; and may include the restriction, modification, or abolition of all or any such rights, and in particular, in the case of severalty owners in common fields, the restriction, modification, or abolition of all or any such rights which may be injurious to the general body of the severalty owners (such as the right of a flock-master or the lord of a manor with an exclusive right of sheepwalk), or to the proper cultivation of the land, compensation being made to any person aggrieved either in money, with his consent, or by the grant of a right of equal

value. In this case and in the foregoing cases one would have expected that the compensation should be paid in money, unless the person aggrieved is content to accept the grant of a right of equal value.

5. Upon commons of any kind, the adjustment of rights comprises the settlement of disputes as to boundaries and the "determination" of any rights in the soil or its produce or otherwise, and the settlement of disputes relating to such rights, whether arising between the commoners themselves or between the commoners in relation to the lords, severalty owners, or other persons entitled to the soil," which settlement may be conducive to the interests of all or any class of persons interested in the common. This clause is very obscure, but its intention seems to be that the Commissioners shall be the sole judges in disputes between commoners, or between commoners and owners in matters relating to the ownership of the soil or the exercise of rights upon the common: and

nothing is said about an appeal from their decision in cases of doubt or hardship.

Improvement of Commons.

When a common is regulated, the Commissioners may provide for its improvement by draining, levelling, manuring, planting trees, or otherwise adding to its beauty; and may also provide for the making of bye-laws for keeping order and preventing nuisances, and generally for the management of the common. Some of these things fall within the ordinary jurisdiction of courts-leet, which are regularly kept up in many parts of the country; and in a great number of manors the homage have power by custom to make bye-laws for the regulation of the commons, which are binding upon all the tenants. Such bye-laws may extend to the draining and fencing of the land, the appointment of a common-keeper, the maintenance of the pound, the stinting of rights of pasture, the setting a mark to distinguish the commoner's cattle, the closing a common for the preservation of the grass, settling the amount of fuel to be taken from a waste, and many other details of management; and by the Inclosure Act of 13 Geo. III. c. 81, the lord of the manor, with the consent of three-fourths of the commoners, may lease part of the common to obtain a rent for fences and improvements; and there are many other usages of the kind which rest upon local customs or the authority of general or local Acts of Parliament. It seems expedient, therefore, to provide that, after a common has been regulated under the Act, all other powers of management and improvement shall cease to be exercised, notwithstanding any Act of Parliament, law, custom, or usage to the contrary.

With regard to the important problem, how best to secure the regulation and improvement of commons which will not come under the operation of this Act, it will certainly be found necessary at some time to provide the Commissioners with the power of purchasing estates and interests in commons and other open spaces which may be required for the public recreation. In many cases there will be no need of using such powers. Where there are large classes of persons interested in a suburban common, there may be no reason to expect or fear any action which could impede the public use of the land, and when a common has been regulated under the provisions of the measure now proposed, no inclosure of any kind will be possible without the sanction of Parliament. But considering what different kinds of land are known as commons and required for the public recreation, some of them in the hands of a few private owners, and others subject by custom or statute to be treated in a manner inconsistent with the public use, it cannot be doubted that inclosures or partitions or dealings with the soil may be carried out in a way which will interfere with the enjoyment of the neighbouring population. The difficulty no doubt might be avoided by accepting the present opportunity. If parliamentary powers are given for the purchase of interests in open spaces required for the public use, it should be provided, that every order made under such powers should state what rights of private owners are affected and to what extent, and whether with the consent of such owners. And the Act should provide that no estate or interest in land should be taken or injuriously affected without compensation being paid or secured, the amount in case of difference to be ascertained as if it were compensation for the compulsory taking of land under the Lands Clauses Consolidation Acts, and that if any person should be aggrieved by any determination of the Commissioners, he should have a legal decision thereon in the manner provided by the Inclosure Act, 1845, or in some similar way to be defined in the Act.

The Home Secretary has lately said upon a public occasion, that according to his belief " the practical effect of the Bill will be to put a stop to inclosures: and, in fact, it has been drawn with that object." But there can be no doubt that in the cases which have been mentioned the desired effect cannot be secured unless powers are taken to purchase commons which the proprietors have the right to divide.

APPENDIX.

THE COMMONS BILL, 1876.

Arrangement of Clauses.

Clause.
1. Short title.

Part I.

Law as to the Regulation and Inclosure of Commons.

Applications in relation to Commons.

2. Alternative provisional order for regulation or inclosure of commons.
3. "Regulation of common" includes adjustment of rights and improvement.
4. Explanation of adjustment of rights.
5. Explanation of improvement.
6. "Inclosure" means inclosure in manner provided by the Inclosure Acts.

7. Provisions for the benefit of a neighbourhood applicable alike to orders for regulation and orders for inclosure.

Suburban Commons.

8. Sanitary authorities to be represented in the case of commons in the neighbourhood of towns.

Procedure.

9. Issue of forms by Commissioners.
10. Rules as to application to Commissioners.
    (1.) Publication of notices of application.
    (2.) Manner of application.
    (3.) Evidence to be furnished in support of application.
    (4.) Evidence in relation to benefit of neighbourhood.
    (5.) Evidence in relation to private interests.
    (6.) Duty of Commissioners on application.
11. Rules as to local inquiry.
    (1.) Inspection and public meeting.
    (2.) Notice of meeting.
    (3.) Contents of notice.
    (4.) Publication of notice.
    (5.) Conduct of meeting.
    (6.) Personal inquiries by Assistant Commissioner.
    (7.) Report of Assistant Commissioner to Inclosure Commissioners.
    (8.) Map to accompany report.

Commons. 95

12. Rules as to provisional orders.
    - (1.) Draft provisional order to be framed.
    - (2.) Provisions for benefit of neighbourhood.
    - (3.) Provisions for protection of private interests.
    - (4.) Deposit of draft order for consideration of parties interested.
    - (5.) Consents before provisional order certified to be expedient.
    - (6.) Reservation in favour of freemen interested in common.
    - (7.) Means of obtaining consents.
    - (8.) Power to modify provisional order before expediency certified.
    - (9.) Certificate of expediency of provisional order.
    - (10.) Confirmation of provisional order.
13. Partial application of procedure under Inclosure Acts.

Supplemental Provisions.

14. Provision as to byelaws.
15. Provision as to certain expenses under order for regulation of a common.

Part II.

Amendment of the Inclosure Acts.

Field Gardens and Recreation Grounds.

16. Expenses of clearing, draining, and fencing field gardens.
17. Substituted allotments for recreation grounds and field gardens.

18. Situation of allotments for recreation grounds and field gardens.
19. Amendment of law as to letting field gardens.
20. Application of surplus rents of recreation grounds and field gardens.
21. Reports to be made by managers of recreation grounds and field gardens.
22. Amendment of law as to town and village greens.

General Amendments.

23. Substitution of Summary Jurisdiction Act, 11 & 12 Vict. c. 43. for repealed Act, 7 & 8 Geo. 4. c. 30. in certain sections of the Inclosure Acts.
24. Extension of Sec. 105. of the Inclosure Act, 1845, as to exchanges and partitions.

PART III.

Miscellaneous.

25. Repeal of certain parts of the Inclosure Act, 1845, and amendment of law as to reports.
26. Act not to apply to metropolitan commons.
27. A common regulated under Act not to be inclosed without sanction of Parliament.

Definitions.

28. Definitions.

SCHEDULE.

A BILL FOR FACILITATING THE REGULATION AND IMPROVEMENT OF COMMONS, AND FOR AMENDING THE ACTS RELATING TO THE INCLOSURE OF COMMONS.

A.D. 1876

Whereas by the Inclosure Acts, 1845 to 1868, upon the application and with the consent of such of the persons interested in any common as in the said Acts in that behalf specified, the Inclosure Commissioners are empowered by provisional order under their seal to authorize the inclosure of such common, provided such inclosure is made on such terms and conditions as may appear to the Commissioners to be proper for the protection of any public interests, and provided also that the Commissioners are of opinion that such inclosure would be expedient, having regard as well to the health, comfort, and convenience of the inhabitants of any cities, towns, villages, or populous places in or near any parish in which the land proposed to be inclosed, or any part thereof, may be situate (herein-after included under the expression the benefit of the neighbourhood), as to the advantage of the persons interested in the common to which such application relates (herein-after included under the expression private interests) ; but such provisional order is of no validity until

Preamble.
8 & 9 Vict.
c. 118.

ss. 26, 27.

and unless the Commissioners have in a report to be laid before Parliament certified that in their opinion the inclosure of such common, if made on the terms and conditions in their provisional order expressed, would be expedient, having regard to the benefit of the neighbourhood as well as to such private interests as aforesaid, nor until and unless an Act of Parliament has been passed confirming such order and affirming such certificate as aforesaid, and directing that the proposed inclosure of the common should be proceeded with accordingly :

And whereas by the said Inclosure Acts, information is required to be supplied and inquiries to be made for the purpose of enabling the Inclosure Commissioners to judge of such expediency as aforesaid, but it is desirable to make further provisions for bringing under the notice of the said Commissioners, and of Parliament, any circumstances bearing on the expediency of allowing the inclosure of a common, regard being had, as directed by the said Inclosure Acts, to the benefit of the neighbourhood as well as to private interests :

Vict. And whereas by the said Inclosure Acts the Commissioners are empowered in the case of a common being waste land of a manor to require, and in their provisional order to specify as one of the conditions of inclosure, the appropriation of an allotment for the purposes of exercise and recreation by the inhabitants of the neighbourhood, and also of an allotment for the labouring poor, and it is expedient to give further effect to the provisions relating to the said allotments (in this Act referred to as allotments for recreation grounds and field gardens):

And whereas it is expedient to give further facilities for enabling the Inclosure Commissioners to regulate, improve, stint, and otherwise deal with commons without wholly inclosing and allotting the same in severalty:

Be it enacted by the Queen's most Excellent Majesty, by and with the advice and consent of the Lords Spiritual and Temporal, and Commons, in this present Parliament assembled, and by the authority of the same, as follows:

1. This Act may be cited for all purposes as the Commons Act, 1876. Short title.

Part I.

Law as to the Regulation and Inclosure of Commons.

Applications in relation to Commons.

2. The Inclosure Commissioners may entertain an application made in manner in this Act mentioned for a provisional order— Alternative provisional order for regulation or inclosure of commons.

(1.) For the regulation of a common; or
(2.) For the inclosure of a common;

Further, an application may be made as respects the same common for the regulation of part of such common, specifying the part to be regulated, and for the inclosure of the residue, and in such case the application shall be dealt with as respects such parts as if they were separate commons, with this exception, that the boundaries as proposed in the application of the part to be regulated and the part to be inclosed may be modified by the provisional order.

The Commissioners shall not proceed to carry any application under this Act into effect until it is made to appear to them that the persons making the application represent at least one-third in value of such interests in the common as are proposed to be affected by the provisional order.

"Regulation of common" includes adjustment of rights and improvement.

3. A provisional order for the regulation of a common may provide, generally or otherwise, for the adjustment of rights in respect of such common, and for the improvement of such common, or for either of such purposes, or for any of the things by this Act comprised under the expression "adjustment of rights" or "improvement of a common."

Explanation of adjustment of rights.

4. The adjustment of rights in respect of a common comprises for the purposes of this Act all or any of the following things:

(1.) As respects rights of common of pasture in a common, being waste land of a manor,—the determination of the persons by whom, the stock by which, and the times at which such common of pasture is to be exercised;

(2.) As respects rights of common of turbary, or taking of estovers, or taking gravel, or otherwise interfering with the soil of the common, being waste land of a manor,—the determination of the persons by whom, and the mode in which, and the times at which such rights are to be exercised, also on compensation made to any person aggrieved, either by grant of a right of equal value, or with his consent in writing, in money,—the restriction, modification, or abolition of all or any of such rights which may permanently injure the common;

(3.) As respects rights of common in land which is not waste land of a manor,—the stinting or other determination of such rights, and the persons by whom, and the mode in which, and the times at which such rights are to be exercised, as also on compensation made to any person aggrieved, either by grant of a right of equal value, or with his consent in writing, in money,—the restriction, modification, or abolition of all or any of such rights which may be injurious to the general body of the commoners or to the proper cultivation of the land;

(4.) As respects any common whether it is or is not waste land of a manor,—the determination of the rights and obligations of the lord of the manor, severalty owners, or other person or persons entitled to the soil of such common, as also on compensation made to any person aggrieved, either by grant of a right of equal value, or with his consent in writing, in money, —the restriction, modification, or abolition of all or any of such rights, and in particular in the case of severalty owners, of all or any of such rights which may be injurious to the general body of the severalty owners or to the proper cultivation of the land; and

(5.) Generally as respects any common, whether it is or is not waste land of a manor,—the determination of any rights and settlement of any disputes relating to boundaries, rights in the soil or in the produce of the soil, or otherwise, whether arising between the commoners themselves, or between the commoners in relation to the lords of the manors, severalty owners, or other person or persons entitled to the soil of the common, which settlement may be conducive to the interests of all or any class of persons interested in the common.

5. The improvement of a common comprises or the purposes of this Act all or any of the ollowing things; that is to say,

Commons.

(1.) The draining, manuring, or levelling the common; and
(2.) The planting trees on parts of such common, or in any other way improving or adding to the beauty of the common; and
(3.) The making or causing to be made bye-laws and regulations for the prevention of or protection from nuisances or for keeping order on the common; and
(4.) The general management of such common.

6. A provisional order for the inclosure of a common means a provisional order for inclosing the common as provided by the Inclosure Acts, 1845 to 1868, as amended by this Act.

7. In any provisional order in relation to a common, the Inclosure Commissioners shall, in considering the expediency of the application, take into consideration the question whether such application will be for the benefit of the neighbourhood, and may, with a view to such benefit, insert in any such order all or any of the following terms and conditions (in this Act referred to as statutory provisions for the benefit of the neighbourhood); that is to say,

(1.) That free access is to be secured to any particular points of view; and
(2.) That particular trees or objects of historical interest are to be preserved; and

"Inclosure" means inclosure in manner provided by the Inclosure Acts. Provisions for the benefit of a neighbourhood applicable alike to orders for regulation and orders for inclosure.

(3.) That there is to be reserved, where a recreation ground is not set out, a privilege of playing games or of enjoying other species of recreation at such times and in such manner and on such parts of the common as may be thought suitable, care being taken to cause the least possible injury to the persons interested in the common; and

41 G. 3. c. 109, s. 8.
(4.) That carriage roads, bridle paths, and footpaths over such land are to be set out in such directions as may appear most commodious to the neighbourhood; and

(5.) That any other specified thing is to be done which may be thought equitable and expedient, regard being had to the benefit of the neighbourhood.

Suburban Commons.

Sanitary authorities to be represented in the case of commons in the neighbourhood of towns.
8. Notice of any application under this Act in relation to a common which is situate within six miles of any town or towns (which common so situate is in this Act referred to as a suburban common,) shall be served as soon as may be on the urban sanitary authority or authorities having jurisdiction over such town or towns, and it shall be lawful for the urban sanitary authority of any such town to appear before the Assistant Commissioner on the occasion of his holding a local inquiry as in this Act mentioned, and also to appear before the Inclosure Commissioners,

and to make to him or them, at any time during the proceedings in relation to obtaining a provisional order under this Act, such representations as they may think fit with respect to the expediency or inexpediency of such application, regard being had to the health, comfort, and convenience of the inhabitants of the town over which such authority has jurisdiction, and to propose to him or them such provisions as may appear to such urban sanitary authority to be proper, regard being had as aforesaid.

Any urban sanitary authority entitled to receive notice of an application in relation to a suburban common may, with the sanction of the Inclosure Commissioners, enter into an undertaking to contribute out of their funds for or towards the maintenance of recreation grounds, or of paths or roads, or the doing any other matter or thing for the benefit of their town in relation to the common to which such application relates.

They may also, in relation to any such common, and with such sanction as aforesaid, enter into an undertaking to pay compensation in respect to the rights of commoners, for the purpose of securing greater privileges for the benefit of their town.

An urban sanitary authority may acquire by gift and hold without licence in mortmain on trust for the benefit of their town any suburban common in respect of which they would be entitled to receive notice of any application made to the Inclosure Commissioners in pursuance of this Act, and any rights in such a common.

They may also in the case of any such suburban common purchase and hold as aforesaid, with a view to prevent the extinction of the rights of common, any saleable rights in common or any tenement of a commoner having annexed thereto rights of common.

They may also, with the consent of persons representing at least one-third in value of such interests in a suburban common as aforesaid as are proposed to be affected by the provisional order, make an application to the Inclosure Commissioners for the regulation of such common with a view to the benefit of their town and the improvement of such common.

Where an urban sanitary authority makes an application under this Act with such consent as aforesaid in respect of the regulation of a common, or undertakes to make any contribution or to pay any compensation or make any other payment out of its funds in respect of a common, such urban sanitary authority may, if the Inclosure Commissioners deem it advisable, having regard to the benefit of the neighbourhood as well as to private interests, be invested with such powers of management or other powers as may be expedient.

The expenses incurred by an urban sanitary authority in pursuance of this section may be defrayed out of any rate applicable to the payment of expenses incurred by such authority in the execution of the Public Health Act, 1875, and not otherwise provided for.

A town for the purposes of this section means any municipal borough, or Improvement Act district, or Local Government district, having a population of not less than five thousand inhabitants.

The population of any town for the purposes of this Act shall be reckoned according to the last publishe dcensus for the time being, and distances shall be measured in a direct line from the outer boundary of the town to the nearest point of the suburban common.

Procedure.

9. The Inclosure Commissioners shall from time to time, upon application made by the persons interested in any common, issue in such form as they may deem expedient, information and directions as to the mode in which applications for the regulation or inclosure of commons under the Inclosure Acts, 1845 to 1868, as amended by this Act, are to be made to the Commissioners, with such explanations as they may think fit with respect to the law for the regulation and inclosure of commons, and the persons so interested may apply accordingly in manner directed by the Inclosure Commissioners. *Issue of forms by Commissioners.*

10. The following rules shall be observed with respect to an application to the Inclosure Commissioners for a provisional order for the regulation or inclosure of a common; that is to say, *Rules as to application to Commissioners.*

(1.) The applicants previously to making their *Publication of*

<small>Notices of application.</small>

application shall publish, in such manner as the Inclosure Commissioners may from time to time, by general or special order, direct, an advertisement giving notice of their intention to apply for such provisional order, and shall also serve a like notice on any urban sanitary authority entitled under this Act to receive such notice:

<small>Manner of application.</small>

(2.) The application shall be in writing, accompanied with a map of the common and, if for the regulation of a common, shall express whether the applicants propose that all or certain specified provisions only of this Act for the adjustment of rights or improvement of commons should be put in force in relation to such common, but, subject as aforesaid, an application for the regulation or inclosure of a common shall be in such form and be made in such manner as the Inclosure Commissioners may from time to time direct:

<small>Evidence to be furnished in support of application.</small>

(3.) On making their application in respect of any common, the applicants shall furnish the Inclosure Commissioners, in answer to questions previously submitted or otherwise in such manner as the said Commissioners may from time to time direct, with information bearing on the expediency of the application considered in relation to the benefit of the neighbourhood as well as to private interests:

(4.) The information to be furnished as bearing on the expediency of the application, considered in relation to the benefit of the neighbourhood, shall comprise statements as to the particulars following; that is to say, as to the number and occupation of the inhabitants of the parish or place in which the common is situate; as to the population of the neighbourhood, and the distance of the common from neighbouring towns and villages; as to the intention of the applicants to propose the adoption of all or any of the statutory provisions as defined by this Act for the benefit of the neighbourhood; as to the circumstance of any ground other than the common to which the application relates being available for the recreation of the neighbourhood; and in the case of a common being waste land of a manor, as to the site, extent, and suitableness of the allotments, if any, proposed to be made for recreation grounds and field gardens, or for either of such purposes; and as to any other matter which in the judgment of the Inclosure Commissioners may assist them in forming an opinion

Evidence in relation to benefit of neighbourhood.

as to whether such application ought to be acceded to, having regard to the benefit of the neighbourhood, and if acceded to, as to what statutory provisions as defined by this Act ought to be inserted in the provisional order for the benefit of the neighbourhood:

The Inclosure Commissioners shall also require, in the case of an application for inclosure, special information as to the advantages the applicants anticipate to be derivable from the inclosure of a common as compared with the regulation of a common, also the reasons why an inclosure is expedient when viewed in relation to the benefit of the neighbourhood:

Evidence in relation to private interests.

(5.) The information to be furnished as bearing on the expediency of the application considered in relation to private interests shall comprise statements as to the several particulars following; that is to say, as to the extent and nature of the common to which the application relates; as to the mines, minerals, or valuable strata (if any) under the same; as to the questions of boundary (if any) concerning such common, or such mines, minerals, or strata; as to the parties interested in such common, and the numbers and proportion in value of interest who have consented to or dissented from the application; as to the nature of the rights requiring the intervention of the Inclosure Commissioners or the interference of Parliament; as to the supposed advantages of the application being acceded to; as to (in cases where the interest of any lord of the manor in the soil of a common or in mineral or other rights may be affected by the provisional order applied for) the allotment (if any) or compensation agreed on or proposed to be made to such lord of the manor in respect of his interest so affected; and as to any other matter which in the judgment of the Inclosure Commissioners may assist them in forming an opinion as to whether such application ought to be acceded to having regard to private interests, and if acceded to as to what provisions ought to be inserted in the provisional order for the protection of private interests:

(6.) The Inclosure Commissioners shall take into consideration any application made to them as in this Act provided, and if satisfied by the information furnished to them as aforesaid, or by any further inquiries made by

Duty of Commissioners on application.

themselves or an Assistant Commissioner, that a primâ facie case has been made out, and that, regard being had to the benefit of the neighbourhood as well as to private interests, it is expedient to proceed further in the matter, they shall order a local inquiry to be held by an Assistant Commissioner.

Rules as to local inquiry.

11. The following rules shall be observed with respect to a local inquiry held by order of the Inclosure Commissioners.

Inspection and public meeting.

(1.) The Assistant Commissioner appointed to hold such inquiry shall inspect the common to which the application relates, and shall convene a public meeting at a suitable time and place for securing the attendance of the neighbouring inhabitants, and of all persons interested in the common.

Notice of meeting.

(2.) Previously to holding such meeting the Assistant Commissioner shall give not less than twenty-one days' notice of his intention to hold the same.

Contents of notice.

(3.) The notice shall, in such form as the Inclosure Commissioners from time to time direct, state the nature of the application made, the objects of the meeting, that the meeting is a public one and held for the purpose of enabling the Assistant Commissioner to hear all persons desirous of being

Commons. 113

heard on the subject matter of the application, whether considered in relation to the benefit of the neighbourhood or to private interests, and the desirability of the attendance of all persons interested in the subject matter of the inquiry.

(4.) The notice shall be given—

    (*a.*) By affixing a copy thereof on the principal door of the church of the parish in which the common to which the application relates, or the greater part thereof, is situate; and

    (*b.*) By posting copies of the same on or near the common to which it relates; and

    (*c.*) By advertising in such manner as the Inclosure Commissioners may direct, or otherwise giving notice of the meeting in such a manner as they think best calculated to ensure publicity in the locality.

<small>Publication of notice.</small>

(5.) The Assistant Commissioner shall preside and regulate the proceedings at such meeting, and shall hear all persons desirous of being heard in relation to the subject matter of the inquiry. He may adjourn any such meeting from time to time, or from place to place, on giving such notice

<small>Conduct of meeting.</small>

of adjournment as he thinks best calculated to ensure publicity.

(6.) The Assistant Commissioner shall also make any inquiries and do any other acts which he may be instructed by the Inclosure Commissioners or may think it advisable to do, for the purpose of enabling the Commissioners to judge as to the expediency of making the provisional order applied for, also as to the nature of the provisions to be inserted in any such provisional order if made.

(7.) The Assistant Commissioner shall report in writing to the Inclosure Commissioners the result of the local inquiry, and of the public meeting or meetings held by him (in such form and with such details as the Inclosure Commissioners may from time to time direct), and specially shall report to the Inclosure Commissioners the information obtained by him as to the several particulars in respect of which the applicants for a provisional order are by this Act required to furnish information to the Inclosure Commissioners.

He shall also report the number of persons who attended the meetings held by him, the objections (if any) made to the application, and the suggestions (if any) made in relation to the provisions to be inserted in the provisional order for the benefit of the neighbourhood or for the protection of private interests, and any other circumstances which he may think expedient, with a view to enable the Inclosure Commissioners to judge of the expediency of making the provisional order, having regard as aforesaid, and also, if the order be made, of the provisions to be inserted therein.

(8.) The report shall be accompanied by an outline or other map on such scale and of such a description as may be directed by the Inclosure Commissioners, with a sketch in the case of an inclosure of a common being waste of land, of a manor, of the allotments (if any) proposed to be made for recreation grounds and field gardens, or for either of such purposes. *Map to accompany report.*

12. The following rules shall be observed with respect to provisional orders to be made by the Inclosure Commissioners; that is to say, *Rules as to provisional orders.*

(1.) The Inclosure Commissioners, if satisfied by the report of the Assistant Commissioner or by further inquiries to be made by themselves or an Assistant Commissioner, that having regard to the benefit of the neighbourhood as *Draft provisional order to be framed.*

well as to private interests, it is expedient to proceed further in the matter, shall frame, in such form and with such provisions as they, having regard as aforesaid, may think expedient, and as are consistent with law and the description of provisional order applied for, a draft provisional order for the consideration of the persons interested in the common, specifying, if such application is for the regulation of a common, whether all or any one or more of the provisions of this Act for the adjustment of rights and the improvement of a common are to be put in force:

Provisions for benefit of neighbourhood.

(2.) With respect to provisions for the benefit of the neighbourhood, there shall be inserted in such draft provisional order all or any of the statutory provisions as defined by this Act for the benefit of the neighbourhood as the Inclosure Commissioners may think expedient; also, if the order is an inclosure order in the case of a common being waste land of a manor, the quantity and situation of the allotments (if any) to be made for recreation grounds and field gardens:

Provisions for protection of private interests.

(3.) With respect to private interests, there shall be inserted in such draft provisional order, (1) where the interest of any lord of the manor in the soil of a common or in mineral or other rights may be affected by the order, a statement of the allotment (if any) or other compensation to be allotted or made to the lord of such manor in respect of his interest so affected; and (2) where there is any mineral property or other rights in relation thereto belonging to persons other than the lord of the manor which may be affected by the order, such provisions and reservations as are required to be inserted by the Inclosure Acts, 1845 to 1868, or as may appear to the Inclosure Commissioners proper to be inserted; also, if there are any other rights which appear to the Commissioners proper to be specially provided for or to be excepted from the operation of the order, there shall be specified the provisions or exceptions to be made in that behalf:

(4.) As soon as may be after making their draft provisional order, the Inclosure Commissioners shall cause a copy thereof to be deposited in the parish in which the common or the greater part thereof is situate to which such order relates, in order that the same may be considered by the parties interested therein, and they shall give

Deposit of draft order for consideration of parties interested.

notice, in such manner as they think best calculated to secure publicity, of such deposit having been made, and of their intention to certify the expediency of such order if the necessary consents are obtained thereto:

<small>Consents before provisional order certified to be expedient.
8 & 9 Vict. c. 118, ss. 27, 29.</small>

(5.) The Inclosure Commissioners shall not certify the expediency of a draft provisional order unless they are satisfied that persons representing at least two thirds in value of such interests in the common as are affected by the order consent thereto; and when the common to which the order relates is the waste land of any manor, or land within any manor to the soil of which the lord of such manor is entitled in right of his manor, then, unless there is more than one person interested in such manor according to the definition of the Inclosure Act, 1845, the Commissioners shall not certify the expediency of the same, unless the person interested in the common in right of such manor, or his substitute under the said Inclosure Act, 1845, consent to such order; and where there is more than one person interested in such manor the Commissioners shall not certify the expediency of the order, in case such persons or the majority of such persons in respect of interest signify their dissent within a time to be limited by the Commissioners:

(6.) Where the freemen, burgesses, or inhabitant householders of any city, borough, or town are entitled to rights of common or other interest in the common to which the draft provisional order relates, the Inclosure Commissioners shall not certify the expediency of such order unless it appears to the Commissioners that two thirds in number of such of the freemen and burgesses so entitled as may be resident in such city, borough, or town, or within seven miles thereof, or of such inhabitant householders, as the case may be, have consented to the order; and in case two thirds in number of such resident freemen and burgesses, or of such inhabitant householders, have so consented, such consent shall be deemed the consent of the class of freemen, burgesses, or inhabitant householders, as the case may be, so entitled: *8 & 9 Vict. c. 118, s. 27. Reservation in favour of freemen interested in common.*

(7.) The Inclosure Commissioners may cause a meeting or meetings to be held by an Assistant Commissioner for the purpose of obtaining the necessary consents, or of ascertaining the interests of consenting or dissenting parties, or they may cause such consents *Means of obtaining consents.*

or dissents to be ascertained in such other manner as they may think fit:

Power to modify provisional order before expediency certified.

(8.) The Inclosure Commissioners may, at any time before certifying the expediency of a draft provisional order, modify the same of their own mere notion, or on the suggestion of any parties interested, but such modifications shall not be of any validity unless they are consented to in the same manner as if they formed part of the draft provisional order originally deposited by the Commissioners:

Certificate of expediency of provisional order.

(9.) When the necessary consents have been obtained to any draft provisional order as originally deposited, or as modified in pursuance of this Act, such order shall be deemed to be final; and the Inclosure Commissioners shall in a report or reports to be made from time to time, as respects each provisional order which has become final as aforesaid, certify that it is expedient that such provisional order should be confirmed by Parliament, together with their reasons for certifying such expediency, and specially, as respects each provisional order, they shall, in such manner as they think best adapted to enable Parliament to judge of the expediency of such order, state the information furnished to them as to the several particulars in respect of which the applicants for a provisional order are by this Act required to furnish information to the Commissioners; also the result of the local inquiry, and of the number and description of the persons who attended the meetings held during such inquiry, and the nature of the objections (if any) made to the application, and the suggestions (if any) made in relation to the provisions to be inserted for the benefit of the neighbourhood or for the protection of private interests by the persons so attending, and any other circumstances which the Commissioners may think it expedient to state for such purposes as aforesaid:

10.) Every report made by the Inclosure Commissioners certifying the expediency of any provisional order under this Act shall be presented to Parliament, and if at any time thereafter it is enacted by Act of Parliament that any order for the regulation or inclosure of a common, the expediency of which has been so certified by the Commissioners, shall be confirmed, the regulation or inclosure of any common to which any such order relates shall be proceeded with and completed ac-

Confirmation of provisional order.
8 & 9 Vict. c.118, s.32.

cording to the terms of the provisional order relating to such common, and to the provisions of the Inclosure Acts, 1845 to 1868, as amended by this Act, and any Act of Parliament containing such enactments as aforesaid shall be deemed to be a public general Act; but a provisional order, until such Act of Parliament as aforesaid has been passed in relation thereto, shall not be of any validity whatever.

Partial application of procedure under Inclosure Acts.

13. The Inclosure Commissioners may insert in any provisional order for the regulation of a common any provisions they may deem necessary for the purpose of carrying such order into effect; but, subject as aforesaid, when an Act of Parliament has been passed as aforesaid, enacting that the regulation of a common shall be proceeded with, the subsequent proceedings for carrying into effect the regulation of such common shall be the same, so far as is practicable, as they would be in case such common were to be inclosed instead of being regulated, and the provisions of the Inclosure Acts, 1845 to 1868, as amended by this Act, shall apply accordingly.

Supplemental Provisions.

Provision as to byelaws.

14. Any byelaw made in pursuance of this Act, and any alteration made therein, and any revocation of a byelaw, shall not be of any validity until it has been confirmed by one of Her Majesty's Principal Secretaries of State.

Pecuniary penalties (to be recovered summarily before any two justices) may be imposed by any such byelaws on persons breaking the same, provided that no penalty exceeds for any one offence the sum of *forty shillings*.

15. Subject to the terms of the provisional order the amount of any compensation to be paid for any restriction, modification, or abolition of rights in pursuance of an order for the regulation of a common shall be deemed to be expenses of and incidental to the regulation of the common, and may be defrayed accordingly. *Provision as to certain expenses under order for regulation of a common.*

Part II.

Amendment of the Inclosure Acts.

Field Gardens and Recreation Grounds.

16. Whereas it is expedient that the expenses of clearing any allotments made for field gardens may be included in the expenses of an inclosure: Be it enacted, that the valuer shall, unless the Inclosure Commissioners otherwise direct, cause every allotment made for a field garden to be cleared, drained, fenced, levelled, and otherwise made fit for immediate use and occupation; and the expenses incurred by the valuer under this section shall be paid as part of the general expenses of the inclosure. *Expenses of clearing, draining, and fencing field gardens.*

17. The provisions of the Inclosure Acts, 1845 to 1868, which authorize the Inclosure Commissioners to allow an equal quantity of the land *Substituted allotments for recreation grounds*

and field gardens.
9 & 10 Vict. c. 70, s. 4. Com. 1869, rec. 12.

proposed to be inclosed to be allotted for the purpose of a recreation ground or field garden, or for any other public purpose, in lieu of that directed to be allotted by any provisional order, shall extend to authorize them to allow the allotment of land of equal value although it may not be of equal quantity.

Situation of allotments for recreation grounds and field gardens.
8 & 9 Vict. c. 118, s. 74.

18. Every allotment made for the purpose of a recreation ground or field garden shall be in such part of the land proposed to be inclosed as appears to the Inclosure Commissioners to be best suited for the purpose for which it is appropriated, and where any land proposed to be inclosed consists partly of common being waste land of a manor (in this section referred to as the first-mentioned land), and partly of common not being waste land of a manor (in this section referred to as the second-mentioned land), and the Commissioners are satisfied that it would be advantageous that the allotment for a recreation ground or a field garden, or any part thereof, should be made out of the second-mentioned land instead of out of the first-mentioned land, the Commissioners may, in the provisional order relating to such land, specify as one of the terms and conditions of the inclosure thereof that the said allotments or the said part thereof shall be made accordingly out of the second-mentioned land, and shall out of the first-mentioned land allot land of equal value by way of exchange to the persons interested in the second-mentioned land.

19. Whereas by the Inclosure Act, 1845, allotment wardens are required to let the allotments under their management to the poor inhabitants of the parish in gardens not exceeding a quarter of an acre, and are further required to demand in respect of such letting, a rent not below the full yearly value of the land to be ascertained in manner in the said Act mentioned; and whereas it is expedient to amend the said provisions: Be it enacted that allotment wardens, if they are unable to let the allotments under their management, or any portion thereof, to the poor inhabitants of the parish in gardens not exceeding a quarter of an acre, may let the same, or any unlet portion thereof, in gardens not exceeding half an acre each, to such inhabitants as aforesaid: Further, it shall be the duty of allotment wardens to offer the gardens under their management to the poor inhabitants of the parish at a fair agricultural rent instead of at such rent as is required by the said Act. Moreover, if in any parish the allotment wardens are unable to let the allotments under their management, or any portion thereof, to the poor inhabitants of the parish in such quantities and at such rents as aforesaid, they may let the same, or such portion as may be unlet, to any person whatever at the best annual rent which can be obtained for the same, without any premium or fine, and on such terms as may enable the allotment wardens to resume possession thereof within a period not exceeding twelve months, if it should at any

Amendment of law as to letting field gardens.

8 & 9 Vict. c. 118, s. 109.

K

time be required for such poor inhabitants as aforesaid.

This section shall apply to any allotment under the management of allotment wardens, in pursuance of the Inclosure Acts, whether made before or after the passing of this Act.

<small>Application of surplus rents of recreation grounds and field gardens.
8 & 9 Vict. c. 118, ss. 73, 112.</small>

20. Whereas by section seventy-three of the Inclosure Act, 1845, the surplus rents arising from recreation grounds are applicable in aid of the rates for the repair of the public highways in the parish or respective parishes in which the said grounds are situate, and by section one hundred and twelve of the same Act the surplus rents arising from field gardens are payable to the overseers of the poor in aid of the poor rates of the parish: And whereas it is expedient to amend the said provisions: Be it enacted, that the surplus rents arising from recreation grounds shall from and after the passing of this Act cease to be applied in manner provided by the said seventy-third section, and shall be applied to all or any of the following purposes, and to no other purpose; that is to say, in improving the recreation grounds or any of them in the same parish or neighbourhood, or maintaining the drainage and fencing thereof, or in hiring or purchasing additional land for recreation grounds in the same parish or neighbourhood; and the surplus rents arising from field gardens shall, from and after the passing of this Act, cease to be applied in manner provided by the said one hundred and twelfth section, and shall be applied to all or any

of the following purposes, and to no other purpose; that is to say, in improving the field gardens or any of them in the same parish or neighbourhood, or maintaining the drainage and fencing thereof, or in hiring or purchasing additional land for field gardens in the same parish or neighbourhood.

21. The trustees of recreation grounds, where such trustees are the overseers or churchwardens of a parish, and the allotment wardens of field gardens shall, from time to time, and at such intervals of not less than three years nor more than five years, as the Inclosure Commissioners direct, make such reports to the said Commissioners in respect of the recreation grounds and field gardens under their management, with such particulars of the rents received by them, as the Commissioners may require. *Reports to be made by managers of recreation grounds and field gardens.*

22. Whereas by the Inclosure Act, 1857, provision is made for the protection of town and village greens, and recreation grounds, and it is expedient to amend such provision: Be it enacted as follows, that is to say, an encroachment on or inclosure of a town or village green, also any erection thereon or disturbance of the soil thereof which is made otherwise than with a view to the better enjoyment of such town or village green or recreation ground, shall be deemed to be a public nuisance, and if any person does any act in respect of which he is liable to pay damages or a penalty under section twelve of the said Inclosure Act, 1857, he may be summarily con- *Amendment of law as to town and village greens. 20 & 21 Vict. c. 31. s. 12.*

victed thereof upon the information of any inhabitant of the parish in which such town or village green or recreation ground is situate, as well as upon the information of such persons as in the said section mentioned.

This section shall apply only in cases where a town or village green or recreation ground has a known and defined boundary.

General Amendments.

<small>Substitution of Summary Jurisdiction Act, 11 & 12 Vict. c. 43. for repealed Act, 7 & 8 Geo. 4, c. 30, in certain sections of the Inclosure Acts.</small>

23. There shall be repealed so much of section ten of the Inclosure Act, 1848, and of section ten of the Inclosure Act, 1849, and of section thirty-three of the Inclosure Act, 1852, as incorporates or refers to any provisions of the Act of the seventh and eighth years of the reign of King George the Fourth, chapter thirty, intituled " An Act for consolidating and amending the laws in England relative to malicious injuries to property," and which last-mentioned provisions have since been repealed, and in place thereof be it enacted, that—

<small>11 & 12 Vict. c. 99, s. 10. 12 & 13 Vict. c. 83, s. 10. 15 & 16 Vict. c. 79, s. 33.</small>

Any offence under section ten of the Inclosure Act, 1848, and under section ten of the Inclosure Act, 1849, and under section thirty-three of the Inclosure Act, 1852, shall be deemed to be an offence punishable on summary conviction under " The Act of the session of the eleventh and " twelfth years of the reign of Her present Majesty, " chapter forty-three, intituled, ' An Act to facili- " ' tate the performance of the duties of justices " ' of the peace out of sessions within England

"'and Wales with respect to summary convic-
"'tions and orders,'" and the Acts amending
the same: Provided that any penalty or forfeiture incurred shall be applied in manner provided by the said Inclosure Acts, and that any information in relation to any such offence as is mentioned in this section shall be heard, tried, determined, and adjudged before two justices.

24. The provisions of section one hundred and five of the Inclosure Act, 1845, relating to the validity after confirmation of an award of inclosure of the exchanges, and partitions set forth in such award, shall apply to orders of exchange, partition, and division of intermixed lands carried into effect in pursuance of the Inclosure Acts, 1845 to 1868, by separate orders, and not included in an award of inclosure.

Extension of sec. 105 of the Inclosure Act, 1845, as to exchanges and partitions.

Part III.

Miscellaneous.

25. There shall be repealed so much of section thirty of the Inclosure Act, 1845, as prescribes a limit to the quantity of land to be allotted to recreation grounds; also the twenty-fourth, twenty-fifth, twenty-sixth, and twenty-seventh sections of the Inclosure Act, 1845, without prejudice to any proceedings already instituted thereunder, and the Inclosure Commissioners shall not be required to repeat, in their general annual report, any of the particulars in relation to the regulation or inclosure of commons which they

Repeal of certain parts of the Inclosure Act, 1845, and amendment of law as to reports.

may have stated in any other reports made by them in pursuance of this Act in relation to such commons, but they may refer to such other reports, or give a summary thereof or otherwise deal with the same as may be thought expedient.

<small>Act not to apply to metropolitan commons.</small>
26. This Act shall not apply to any metropolitan common within the meaning of the Metropolitan Commons Acts, 1866 and 1869.

<small>A common regulated under Act not to be inclosed without sanction of Parliament.</small>
27. Where an Act of Parliament has been passed confirming a provisional order under this Act for the regulation of a common, then, subject to and without prejudice to the provisions of that order, such common shall not, nor shall any part thereof, be inclosed without the sanction of Parliament subsequently obtained.

Definitions.

<small>Definitions.</small>
28. In this Act, unless the context otherwise requires,—

"A common" means any land subject to be inclosed under the Inclosure Acts, 1845 to 1868:

<small>8 & 9 Vict. c.118, s.30.</small>
"Waste land of a manor" means and includes any land consisting of waste land of any manor on which the tenants of such manor have rights of common, or of any land subject to any rights of common which may be exercised at all times of the year for cattle levant and couchant, or to any rights of common which may be exercised at all times of the year, and are not limited by number or stints: .

"Person" includes a body corporate:

"Inclosure Acts, 1845 to 1868," means the Acts mentioned in the schedule hereto, and each of the acts mentioned in the said schedule may be cited by the short title in such schedule in that behalf mentioned; and the above mentioned Acts together with this Act may be cited as "The Inclosure Acts, 1845 to 1876:"

"Municipal borough" means any place for the time being subject to the Act of the session of the fifth and sixth years of the reign of King William the Fourth, chapter seventy-six, intituled "An Act to provide for the "regulation of municipal corporations in "England and Wales," and the Acts amending the same:

"Improvement Act district" means any area subject to the jurisdiction of any commissioners, trustees, or other persons invested by any local Act of Parliament with powers of improving, cleansing, lighting, or paving any town:

"Local government district" has the same meaning as it has in the Public Health Act, 1875.

SCHEDULE.

Year and Chapter.	Title.	Short Title.
8 & 9 Vict. c. 118.	An Act to facilitate the inclosure and improvement of commons and lands held in common, the exchange of lands, and the division of intermixed lands; to provide remedies for defective or incomplete executions, and for the non-execution of the powers of general and local Inclosure Acts, and to provide for the revival of such powers in certain cases.	The Inclosure Act, 1845.
9 & 10 Vict. c. 70.	An Act to amend the Act to facilitate the inclosure and improvement of commons.	The Inclosure Act, 1846.
10 & 11 Vict. c. 111.	An Act to extend the provisions of the Act for the inclosure and improvement of commons.	The Inclosure Act, 1847.
11 & 12 Vict. c. 99.	An Act to further extend the provisions of the Act for the inclosure and improvement of commons.	The Inclosure Act, 1848.
12 & 13 Vict. c. 83.	An Act further to facilitate the inclosure of commons and the improvement of commons and other lands.	The Inclosure Act, 1849.
14 & 15 Vict. c. 53.	An Act to consolidate and continue the Copyhold and Inclosure Commissions, and to provide for the completion of proceedings under the Tithe Commutation Acts.	The Inclosure Commissioners Act, 1851.

Year and Chapter.	Title.	Short Title.
15 & 16 Vict. c. 79.	An Act to amend and further extend the Acts for the inclosure, exchange, and improvement of land.	The Inclosure Act, 1852.
17 & 18 Vict. c. 97.	An Act to amend and extend the Acts for the inclosure, exchange, and improvement of land.	The Inclosure Act, 1854.
20 & 21 Vict. c. 31.	An Act to explain and amend the Inclosure Acts.	The Inclosure Act, 1857.
22 & 23 Vict. c. 43.	An Act to amend and extend the provisions of the Acts for the inclosure, exchange, and improvement of land.	The Inclosure Act, 1859.
31 & 32 Vict. c. 89.	An Act to alter certain provisions in the Acts for the commutation of tithes, the Copyhold Acts, and the Acts for the inclosure, exchange, and improvement of land, and to make provision towards the expense of the Copyhold, Inclosure and Tithe Office.	The Inclosure, &c. Expenses Act, 1868.